☆ INSIGHT COMPACT GUIDE

BaTH
& SURROUNDINGS

Compact Guide: Bath & Surroundings is the ultimate quick-reference guide to this world-famous city. It tells you everything you need to know about Bath's attractions, from ancient baths to elegant squares and crescents, through fascinating museums to beautiful waterways and gardens.

This is one of 133 Compact Guides, which combine the interests and enthusiasms of two of the world's best known information providers: Insight Guides, whose titles have set the standard for visual travel guides since 1970, and Discovery Channel, the world's premier source of nonfiction television programming.

APA PUBLICATIONS
Part of the Langenscheidt Publishing Group

Star Attractions

An instant reference to some of Bath's most popular tourist attractions to help you on your way.

The Great Bath p19

Royal Crescent p22

Bath Abbey p20

Assembly Rooms p24

Bradford-on-Avon p37

Wells Cathedral p46

Longleat p52

Stonehenge p54

Stourhead p54

Introduction

Places

Culture

Leisure

Practical Information

Bath – A Georgian Jewel

Bath makes a striking first impression, especially on anyone approaching the city from the heights of Lansdown, Swainswick or Claverton. The configuration of crescents, squares and terraces that unfolds below is a triumphant expression of the Augustan Age of Reason. Here order and precision combine with lightness and grace, satisfying both the mind and the senses. But Bath is not only famed for its superb Georgian architecture; at its elegant heart are the Roman baths, the most impressive Roman remains in Britain with the exception of Hadrian's Wall.

Location, population and economy

The city lies cradled in the Mendip Hills, the source of its famous pale stone as well as the hot springs that have been its *raison d'être* since Celtic times. Dissected by the Avon river, which flows into the Severn estuary at Avonmouth, the Kennet and Avon Canal (1810) and the Great Western Railway (1841), the city covers 11 hilly sq miles (29sq km). It centres on the ancient Abbey and Roman Baths, with Georgian Bath spreading north to the Upper Town and east over the river to Bathwick.

Aerial view of the Upper Town
The Roman Great Bath

5

The city has 84,000 inhabitants, though this number is boosted by some 2 million tourists a year, not to mention out-of-towners who come for its shops, restaurants, theatre and concerts. While in many minds the city is associated with middle-class retirees, in actual fact its population is an invigorating mix of young and old. Attracting the former are Bath University, which is strong in science and technology, Bath Spa University College and the City of Bath College.

Music man

Though tourism is important (the Roman Baths are fourth in Britain's league of attractions, after the Tower of London, St Paul's Cathedral and Windsor Castle), publishing also thrives, along with information technology industries, which have spawned along the whole of the M4 corridor. There are also hopes of reviving Bath's reputation as a spa. In 2003 the city opened new spa facilities, utilising the hot springs for the first time since 1976. The superb modern complex based on the historic baths at the top of Bath Street offers up-to-the-minute health and beauty treatments.

Bath has long been a magnet for artists, musicians and craftspeople. It also attracts a large number of vagrants, whose begging prompts sporadic protest as far away as Westminster. There is nothing very new in this: in the 16th century two acts of Parliament concerning vagrancy specifically mentioned Bath.

Bristol Channel

○ Bath

English Channel

*UNESCO symbol outside
the Pump Room*

*A stylish busker
Gorgon head, the Roman Baths*

World Heritage Site

In 1988, Bath was designated a World Heritage Site by UNESCO. This means it is considered a site of outstanding historical importance; its 'loss, through deterioration or disappearance...constitutes an impoverishment of the heritage of all the peoples of the world'. As such it is eligible for grants from the World Heritage Fund to help preserve its buildings.

Key defenders of the city's heritage are Bath City Council's Conservation Committee and the Bath Preservation Trust, a long-established body which monitors the council's work and keeps it on its toes. Their work ranges from major restorations of historic buildings (of which there are almost 5,000), such as Beckford's Tower on Lansdown Hill, to ensuring even the smallest repair to a listed structure – from a drain grille to a bell pull – is as far as possible in keeping with the Georgian original. This has led to some well-publicised battles between the Trust and local residents, including one concerning a yellow door (instead of the prescribed white or stripped wood) in the Royal Crescent. Arbitration was eventually referred to the House of Lords, who ruled in favour of the resident.

There is also a conflict of interests between excavating the archaeological remains and preserving the city's fine Georgian heritage. The Roman baths we see today are just a small portion of the total Roman complex, which is believed to extend for 24 acres (10 hectares) about 20ft (6m) below the Georgian city. Though inspired by classical ideals, the Georgian architects were not very interested in unearthing ancient ruins and simply built over the top of them. Many mysteries therefore perplex the Bath Archaeological Trust. Where, for example, is the location of the *tholos* (circular temple) to which stone blocks discovered in the 19th century undoubtedly belonged? (Prob-

ably, beneath the front of the Abbey.) And where are the Roman fort and theatre which almost certainly existed? Modern-day archaeological projects try to be sensitive to both the Georgian and Roman heritage. Excavation of the Temple Precinct beneath the Pump Room in 1981–83 was a brilliant achievement, with Roman and Georgian interests both being served at once. There is an ongoing programme of further archaeological excavations.

Bath and the Romans

Julius Caesar invaded Britain in 55 BC, landing at Dover and moving into Kent. However, the island was not conquered properly until 43–83 AD, when Roman forces, establishing a network of forts and military roads, spread west into Wales and north into Scotland (then called Caledonia). Though repelled by fierce and ongoing resistance by the Scottish tribes and the Picts of northern England, resulting in the building of Hadrian's Wall in around AD 120, the legions' progress was generally swift and easy, not least on account of the willingness of the Romans to embrace local Celtic culture.

Cooling down in summer

The Romans arrived in Bath in the middle of the first century AD, founding Aquae Sulis on the site of a Druid grove surrounding the sacred hot springs of Sula, a Celtic goddess associated with wisdom and healing. Adapting the local cult, they built a temple to Sulis Minerva, a blend of Sulis and her Roman counterpart, Minerva.

A book-binder at work

By the third century the temple and its baths were attracting pilgrims from all over the Roman Empire, who would come to petition the goddess and bathe in the healing waters. The baths were also a social centre, with steam rooms equipped with hypocaust flooring, a sauna, a cold plunge pool and alcoves for massage and beauty treatments such as hair removal. A community grew around the temple; local people found employment in the baths or in the pewter industry which alloyed tin from Cornwall with lead from the Mendip Hills.

By the fourth century the Romans were losing control of Britain. As Barbarian attacks from northern Europe grew in intensity, travel became dangerous, leading to a decline in trade at the baths. Christianity was also gaining hold, putting an end to the cult of Sulis Minerva.

Bath and the Georgians

Until the early 18th century Bath was not an elegant city. Though a popular spa, it had a mixed reputation. It was occasionally visited by royalty, but it was also a magnet for the diseased poor, bogus doctors and conmen galore. Lodging-houses were cramped or squalid, the streets were plagued by thieves and the entertainments laid on for visitors were considered provincial. The spa also had a rep-

Pulteney Bridge at night and Beau Nash

utation for licentiousness – the act of undressing for the baths seeming to loosen visitors' morals as well as their whalebone stays.

The city's transformation into one of the most beautiful cities in Europe is generally attributed to the combined talents of three self-made men: Richard (Beau) Nash, a charismatic dandy; Ralph Allen, an astute businessman; and John Wood, a trail-blazing architect.

A key date in the city's metamorphosis was 1705 when Nash was made the Master of Ceremonies following the death in a duel of the previous incumbent. Though a professional gambler, Nash was a born organiser with immense personal charm. On assuming his new post he took immediate measures to improve the spa's facilities. Financing projects by subscriptions, he introduced street cleaning and lighting, commissioned the building of assembly rooms, and regulated the trade of the sedan chairmen.

Nash also laid down a code of behaviour for visitors. As well as banning swords, white aprons and riding boots from the new assembly rooms, the code stated that 'all whisperers of lies and scandal be taken for their authors' and that 'the elder ladies and children be content with a second bench at the ball, as being past or not come to perfection' – a pronouncement that may have coined the expression 'wall-flower'.

Ralph Allen was also crucial to the meteoric rise of the West Country spa town. As well as being one of the founders of the modern post office (until Allen's reforms, the postal system was corrupt as well as inefficient), he was the first to exploit the quarries of nearby Combe Down, thus introducing the honey-coloured stone that was to become the city's hallmark. Allen was also a patron of the arts and invited many of the brightest minds of the day to parties at Prior Park, his mansion (now a

The fine art of flirting

National Trust property, *see page 44*) near Combe Down, thus adding intellectual zest to the increasingly rich Bath mix. Alexander Pope, Henry Fielding, Gainsborough, and the actors James Quin and David Garrick were among his regular guests.

The third great, and today most visible, influence on Bath was John Wood, who introduced the Palladian style of architecture inspired by ancient Greece and Rome (*see page 61*). At just 23 years of age, Wood sent Allen an ambitious plan for Bath's development, in anticipation of the massive building boom to come. Though this was not taken up, Wood soon joined forces with the speculator Robert Gay. His first great achievement was Queen Square, 1728–1735, followed by the North and South Parades. His son, John Wood the Younger, assumed his father's mantle, transforming the Upper Town with the Royal Crescent, the Circus and the New Assembly Rooms.

The elegant environment which these men created drew the cream of fashionable society from 1705 until the late 1750s. But the wider craze for Bath reached its zenith between 1760 and 1795, during the reign of George III.

Dressed for the part, c. 1745

Bath's main 'season' was September to May, with most visitors staying between six weeks and three months. From the moment the bells in Bath Abbey peeled out to welcome them (the bells announced all new arrivals of any social significance) to the morning their luggage was loaded on the coach for their arduous journey home, their days were filled with bathing, visiting acquaintances, seeing plays and attending balls. For most people, each morning began with a dip in the baths followed by a turn around the Pump Room and then breakfast in the Assembly Rooms. The rest of the morning might be spent attending a church service followed by a stroll along the parades, and the afternoon at the shops, coffee houses or gaming tables. Twice a week a ball was held at one or other of the assembly rooms; other nights might be spent at the theatre, where during the 1770s Sarah Siddons held audiences spellbound, or at a concert, perhaps given by the celebrated castrato Venanzio Rauzzini, for whom Mozart wrote *Exsultate Jubilate* in 1774. Newcomers to Bath could learn about amenities from a growing number of guidebooks to the city.

The Octagon in the Assembly Rooms

At the end of the 18th century Bath began to lose its lustre, as the upper classes deserted to Tunbridge Wells, Cheltenham and later Brighton, where George IV while Prince Regent had built the flamboyant Pavilion. Bath turned into a residential city favoured by the professional classes in search of a comfortable but inexpensive living. Jane Austen lived in several properties in Bath from 1801–06. Her novel *Persuasion*, published in 1820 and partly set in the city, depicts a city populated by colonels and captains disbanded from the Napoleonic Wars.

Jane Austen's house, 1804

Historical Highlights

5000BC Nomads hunt deer, wild pigs and ox in the area.

4000–3000BC Settlements evolve and the Avon valley is a natural conduit for the flow of ideas and trade. The oldest parts of Stonehenge date to this time.

2000–12000BC Bronze Age. Round barrow burials in surrounding area. The Monkswood Hoard, a collection of bronze items found during the construction of Monkswood Reservoir, date from the end of this period (they are displayed in the Pump Room).

1000BC Celtic peoples arrive from France and the Low Countries.

AD43 The Romans invade Britain under Emperor Claudius. In the marshy area of Bath, they find Celts worshipping a water goddess called Sulis. They name the place Aquae Sulis. Over the next 30 years they build a complex of baths and temples which draw visitors and pilgrims from far and wide. The Romans also mine lead and silver in the Mendip Hills and are the first to quarry the stone of Coombe Down, near Bath.

410 Sustained Barbarian attacks from Ireland and northern Europe force the Romans to withdraw from Britain, which now enters the Dark Ages. The bathing complex falls into disuse.

577 The Battle of Dyrham. Despite a spirited defence by the Britons, Bath is captured by the Saxons, along with Gloucester and Cirencester.

676 King Osric founds a religious establishment at Bath under Abbess Berta and pagan images are destroyed. By the 8th century, a community of monks is in charge. Under their influence, a new town rapidly evolves. Roman buildings are plundered for stone.

973 Edgar, King of all England, is crowned in Bath Abbey. The ceremony is attended by the Archbishop of Canterbury.

1066 The Norman Conquest.

1086 The Doomsday Book records that sheep are the chief livestock in Bath and the region, anticipating the medieval wool trade.

1088 John of Tours becomes Bishop of Wells, and in 1090 transfers the see to Bath where, interested in the medicinal properties of the waters, he builds a hospital. In 1192 the see is split between Bath and Glastonbury and then from 1244 between Bath and Wells.

14th century The wool and weaving industries flourish in Bath and the surrounding region (Chaucer's Wife of Bath is a weaver). They are controlled by the Church.

1499 Work begins on the present Abbey, with William Vertue, the master mason of Henry VII, engaged to work on the fan vaulting. Building is brought to a sudden halt 40 years later by the Dissolution of the Monasteries (1539).

16th century Bath regains its reputation as a spa and new baths and hospitals are built. Increasing numbers of beggars flock to Bath prompting an Act of Parliament in 1572 to restrict their number. Meanwhile the abbey is rescued from dereliction by Elizabeth I, who starts a nationwide collection.

1618–48 The Thirty Years' War damages cloth exports to Germany. Hardship among wool and clothmakers ensues. However, the industry doesn't sink yet; it turns to the home market.

1642 The Civil War between the Parliamentarians and the Royalists. Bath initially sides with the Parliamentarians but switches sides several times and eventually supports the Royalists.

1660 The monarchy is restored.

1685 Monmouth's protestant rebellion is put down.

1702 Queen Anne visits Bath to take the waters, thus accelerating a growing trend.

1706 Beau Nash becomes Master of Ceremonies and makes many improvements to the facilities at Bath, gradually transforming the town into England's most fashionable resort.

1715 The coronation of George I.

1727 The gilded bronze head of Minerva is discovered under Stall Street. It is the first clue to the Roman ruins below the Georgian city, but no further explorations are made. Around the same time Ralph Allen begins quarrying stone at Combe Down and constructs a small railway to bring the blocks into town.

1739 and 1749 Laws clamp down on gambling, one of the main pastimes in Bath, and some card games are banned. These measures have a detrimental effect on Beau Nash, who makes his living from playing cards.

1742 The General Hospital (now the Royal Mineral Hospital), intended for the visiting poor, is completed. Its instigator William Oliver becomes its chief physician.

1754–74 The Upper Town becomes increasingly fashionable. The Circus, the Royal Crescent and the Assembly Rooms are all built during this period.

1755 Building works reveal further signs of the underlying Roman baths. In 1759 more evidence – the steps of the Great Bath and part of the Gorgon's Head pediment – is found during construction of the new Pump Room.

1761 Beau Nash dies. Succeeding Masters of Ceremonies lack Nash's natural talent for the job.

1787 Plans unfold to develop the land east of Pulteney Bridge. Building work, however, is interrupted by the outbreak of war with France in 1793.

1798–9 Jane Austen writes her first novel, *Northanger Abbey*, much of which is set in Bath.

1801 Population reaches 33,000.

1810 The completion of the Kennet and Avon Canal, linking the Kennet at Newbury with the Avon at Bath, facilitates the passage of iron, stone, coal and agricultural produce between London and Bath and Bristol.

1815–16 Jane Austen writes her last novel, *Persuasion*, also set in Bath.

1832 The Great Reform Act.

1840 Brunel's Great Western Railway is brought through Bath, making access easier for visitors.

1878 Charles Davis, the city surveyor and architect, discovers Roman remains while investigating a leak from the King's Bath. Excavations reveal the full extent of the Great Bath, and further investigations uncover the Circular Bath. Tourists flock to see the amazing finds.

1925 Bath Act. New buildings must be faced with Bath stone or a suitable substitute.

1934 The Bath Preservation Trust is founded.

1942 'Baedeker raids' by the Luftwaffe in retaliation for the British bombing of the historic German cities Lübeck and Rostok. Baedeker guidebooks are reputedly used to identify appropriate targets. Many buildings are destroyed, necessitating a long programme of restoration.

1948 The prestigious International Music Festival is inaugurated.

1950s A programme to clean the blackened buildings begins. Work progresses slowly but steadily until the 1980s.

1966 Bath University is founded.

1971–80 The West Baths are excavated.

1974 Bath is incorporated in the newly created county of Avon.

1976 Spa facilities are closed on health grounds.

1981 The Temple Precinct is excavated beneath the Pump Room.

1987 Bath is designated a world heritage site by UNESCO.

1991 Bath Abbey receives a major face-lift.

1996 The county of Avon is abolished. Bath and Wansdyke become a unitary council.

2003 New spa facilities open.

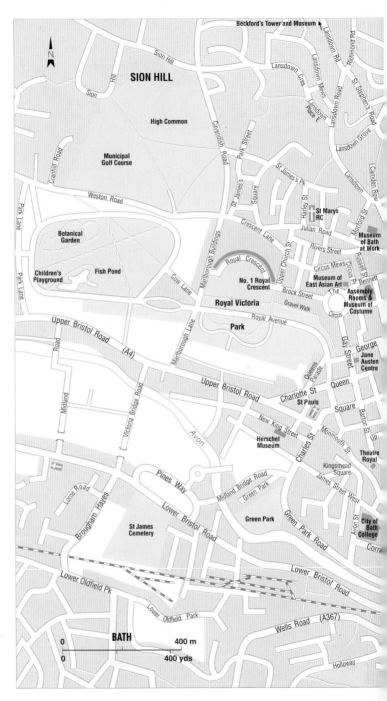

Beckford's Tower and Museum

Lansdown Rd

Richmond Rd

Sion Hill

SION HILL

Lansdown Cres

Lansdown Mews

Lansdown Place E

St Stephen's Road

Lansdown Road

Lansdown Grove

Camden Row

Sion Hill

Sion

High Common

Cavendish Road

Park Street

Municipal Golf Course

St James's Pk

St James's Square

Lansdown

Mortord St

Weston Road

Crescent Lane

Harley St

St Marys RC

Julian Road

Museum of Bath at Work

Russell St

Park Lane

Botanical Garden

Marlborough Buildings

Royal Crescent

Upper Church St

Rivers Street

Circus Mews

Museum of East Asian Art

Circus Pl

Bennett

Children's Playground

Fish Pond

Cow Lane

No. 1 Royal Crescent

Brock Street

The Circus

Assembly Rooms & Museum of Costume

Park Lane

Royal Victoria

Gravel Walk

Royal Avenue

Gay Street

Upper Bristol Road

Park

George

Marlborough Lane

Queens Parade

Jane Austen Centre

Midland Road

Upper Bristol Road (A4)

Upper Bristol Road

Charlotte St

Queen

St Pauls

Square

Barton St

Victoria Bridge Road

Avon

New King Street

Charles St

Monmouth St

Herschel Museum

Kingsmead Square

Theatre Royal

Lorne Road

Pines Way

Midland Bridge Road

James Street West

Green Park

Avon St

City of Bath College

Brougham Hayes

Lower Bristol Road

Green Park

Green Park Road

Corn

St James Cemetery

Lower Bristol Road

Lower Oldfield Pk

Lower Oldfield Park

Wells Road (A367)

Holloway

BATH

0   400 m

0   400 yds

14

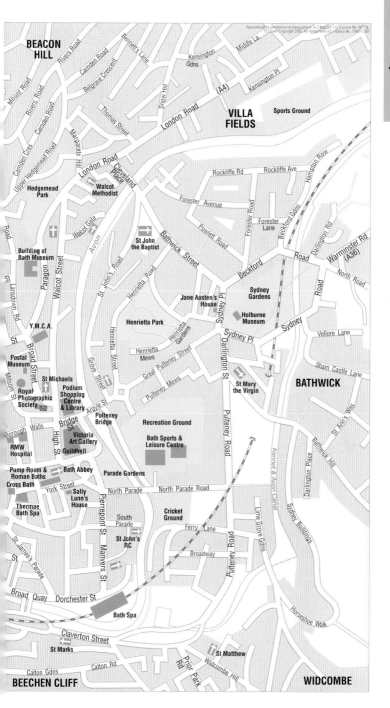

Begin at the Pump Room

Route 1

The Ancient Centre

The Pump Room – Roman Baths – Bath Abbey – Sally Lunn's

The first route focuses on the old core of Bath, the Roman Baths and the medieval Bath Abbey, finishing with a visit to the oldest house in Bath, Sally Lunn's, now a restaurant-cum-teashop with a basement museum.

Tea in the Pump Room

This tour begins at the ★★★ **Pump Room ❶** (Apr–Sept daily 9am–6pm, Oct–Mar daily 9.30am–5pm, Sun 10.30am–5pm; free admission), built between 1790–95 as a replacement for an earlier, smaller pump-room. It was here that the therapeutic waters, pumped directly from the source, could be sampled in comfort. As the doctors of the day recommended taking the waters before breakfast, the Pump Room was open from 6am onwards. It was also a social forum complete with musical entertainment, though not filled with tables and chairs as it is today. In the 1800s the custom was to walk about the room to see and be seen.

Visitors today can walk along the sides of the Pump Room, but it is more pleasant to admire the room over morning coffee, lunch or one of the set afternoon teas while being entertained by the Pump Room Trio (winter 10.30am–12.30pm, summer 10am–12 noon and 3–5pm) or pianist (lunchtime daily).

At the far end of the room, a statue of Beau Nash presides over the scene, flanked by portraits of Catherine Countess of Orford and Sir Robert Walpole, Earl of Orford. Below the statue is the **Tompion clock** showing time, date

Preceding pages: the Great Bath by torchlight

and weather, donated in 1709 by Thomas Tompion, one of England's foremost clockmakers. It is a rare example of a clock with a built-in time equation showing the difference between solar (calculated by the sundial in the end window overlooking the King's Bath) and mean time. Also here are two **sedan chairs**, the main mode of transport in Georgian Bath. The one on the left, with licence plate No 68, would have been hired in the same way as taxis are today; the one topped by a coronet was a private chair.

In the alcove on the south side of the room overlooking the King's Bath, spa water is dispensed (small charge, but free to Bath residents and disabled visitors) from a lovely late 19th-century drinking fountain graced by four stone trout. If you wish to sample the water one glass is probably sufficient to share: in Georgian times, however,

Sample the water

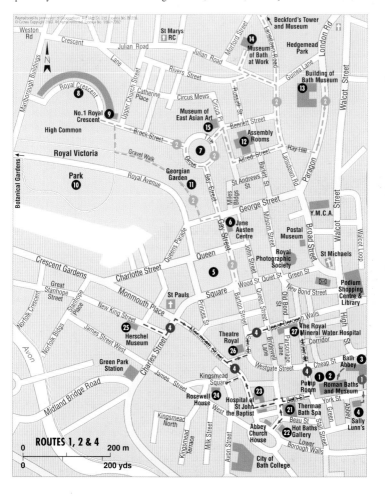

Roman Bath exterior

The head of Minerva

as much as a gallon a day might have been prescribed.

Pass through the **Sun Room** (lined with paintings and cartoons, including an oil portrait of Beau Nash by William Hoare) to the ★★★ **Roman Baths and museum ❷** (Nov–Feb 9.30am–5.30pm, Mar–Jun & Sept–Oct 9am–6pm, Jul & Aug 9am–10pm with torchlight illumination of the Great Bath after 6pm; last admission one hour before closing; admission charge; audio tours provided in six languages). The ticket foyer in the former Concert Room, contains a number of interesting exhibits, including a bath chair, a contraption invented by James Heath in the early 19th century. Requiring only one operator, the bath chair was cheap to run, but it could not provide the same bath-to-bed service as the sedan.

The **Great Bath**, seen below on entering the Roman Baths, was discovered in the 1880s by the city surveyor and architect, Charles Davis, while he was investigating the cause of hot-water floods in local cellars. The Victorians were as excited by archaeology and the past as the Georgians had been indifferent and his discovery was greeted by enormous interest throughout Britain. The colonnade and statues of Roman emperors surrounding the bath, together with the Concert Room (*see above*) were added at the end of the 19th century by J. M. Brydon to appeal to the many tourists who came to see the newly exposed bath.

From here the route leads down to the heart of the baths, the **Temple Precinct**, excavated beneath the Pump Room in the early 1980s. The Temple, one of several in the vicinity, was built in around AD60, on the site of the native Sanctuary of Sulis, a Celtic goddess associated with healing, whom the Romans identified with their own goddess of healing, Minerva. Over a period of years the Romans built an elaborate religious complex complete with curative baths, the magnificence of which they hoped would help convince the native Britons of the benefits of Roman rule.

Finds from the period enliven the excavations, including votive offerings and petitions to the goddess Sulis-Minerva. Over 13,000 coins have been found here, many of them clipped to indicate that they were the property of the goddess and no longer legal tender. Curses, inscribed on pewter or lead sheets, also abound, some written backwards. These generally solicit help or revenge for mundane grievances – the theft of a glove or the heinous case of a stolen napkin ring.

Other highlights in the museum include the gilded **bronze head of Minerva**, minus helmet (you can see the rivet holes where this would have been held in place), discovered in 1727 by workmen in Stall Street and the first intimation of the marvellous Roman ruins below Georgian Bath; the **Gorgon's head** which would have adorned the main Temple's pediment; the corner blocks of a sacrificial altar (the figure of Hercules Bibax on the left and Bachus with a panther on the right) and the Sea Beast mosaic from the floor of a villa near the complex.

Sea Beast mosaic

The museum emerges next to the ★★ **Great Bath**, from where guided tours take in the East and West baths, including the medieval King's Bath. The Great Bath is the best place to see the water at close quarters. Bubbling up at a temperature of 45°C (115°F) and laden with 43 different minerals, including iron which stains the stone red, the water is thought to spring from 2 miles (3 km) beneath the Mendip Hills, on which it fell as rain up to 10,000 years ago. Its green colour is caused by light reacting with algae: when the baths were roofed over, as they were in Roman times, the water would have been clear (a section of the vaulted roof is propped up against the wall at the west end of the Great Bath). The water is continually renewed. Water arrives in the northwest corner, fed from the Sacred Spring, and leaves by a sluice controlled drain, which channels it into the River Avon.

Great Bath and sacred spring

The Great Bath was essentially a swimming bath, with alcoves for beauty treatments and entertainment. The ★★ **East Baths** were for serious ablutions, offering a tepidarium (warm room), where oils and massage were applied, and a calidarium (hot room) with steam. Hypocaust flooring would have provided heating.

The ★★ **West Baths** include more of the same, plus a stoke house and the **Circular Bath**, a cold plunge bath whose waters were piped in specially (all the springs being hot). Also here is the ★★ **King's Bath**, which is overlooked by the Pump Room. In a niche on one side of the bath is a statue of King Bladud, the mythical founder of the city. According to legend, Bladud had suffered from leprosy as a prince and roamed the countryside disguised as a swineherd. His condition was miraculously cured when, observing how the skin of his scabrous swine was improved after wallowing in some hot springs, he plunged in himself. The new, pearly-skinned Bladud was duly rehabilitated by the court and went on to become king and found Bath on the site of the springs. Bladud is commemorated all over the city; the acorns topping the pediment of the Circus, for example, are said to allude to Bladud's period as a swineherd.

The King's Bath was used in the Middle Ages (together with the Cross Bath and the Hot Bath: *see page 31*). It was built on the site of the Roman Sacred Spring by the Norman Bishop John of Tours, whose interest in medicine encouraged him to build an infirmary on the north side of the bath over the old Temple Precinct. The bath itself was furnished with stone seats on which the sick could submerge themselves in the waters. The bronze rings on the sides of the bath were the gifts of grateful patients who had been cured.

King's Bath

From the Baths it is a short walk across Abbey Churchyard to ★★ **Bath Abbey** ❸ (summer 9am–6pm, winter 9am–4,30pm, restricted opening for sight-seeing on Sunday; suggested admission charge), the heart of Bath in the Middle Ages. The introduction of Roman Catholicism by the Saxons was an important factor in Bath's renaissance. In 675 Abbess Berta founded a Convent of Holy Virgins here on land endowed by Osric, a minor Mercian king. Though there is no further record of the convent, there is evidence that a Saxon abbey existed in 781. It was here, in the abbey church, that Edgar, the first king of all England, was crowned in 973. Edgar introduced the Benedictine monks that were to control the abbey, and thus the growing medieval town, for the next 500 years.

In 1107, in the wake of the Norman conquest, the Bishop of Somerset moved the seat of the bishopric from Wells to Bath (a controversial move that eventually led to the Pope renaming the diocese Bath and Wells) and built a Norman church on the site of the Saxon one. This lasted until 1499, when Bishop Oliver King, inspired by a dream, rebuilt the church in the late-English Gothic, or perpendicular, style characterised by flying buttresses, wide windows and fan vaulting.

The Dissolution of the Monasteries by Henry VIII in 1539 brought the work to a halt, leaving the nave without a roof. Its eventual completion is said to have come about nearly a century later after James Montague, Bishop of Bath and Wells, sought shelter here while walking in a storm with Sir John Harrington, a godson of Queen Elizabeth I. According to the story, the rain-soaked Harrington turned to Montague and said, 'If the church does not keep us safe from the water above, how shall it save others from the fires below?', prompting the bishop to commission

Tomb of Bishop Montague and east view of the Abbey

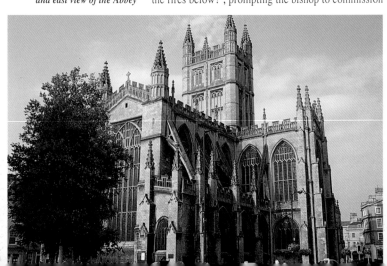

a roof. Records show that Queen Elizabeth I took an interest in the abbey after her visit to the city in 1574, initiating a nationwide appeal for funds.

The entrance to the abbey is through the ★ **West Front**, with its Jacob's Ladder ('the angels of God ascending and descending on it': Genesis 28: 12–17). Inside, the vast windows fill the abbey with light, earning it the epithet 'Lantern of the West' during Elizabethan times. The ★ **east window** depicts 56 scenes in the Life of Christ in brilliant stained glass. Overhead stretches the lovely ★ **fan vaulting**. This was added in two stages: the first (over the chancel) by William Vertue, master mason to Henry VII, when the abbey was built, and the rest in the mid-19th century during restorations by George Gilbert Scott.

Fan vaulting over the nave

Among the delights of the abbey are the ★ **memorials** to famous city residents and guests who died in Bath for want of the desired cure (it is estimated that 3,879 bodies lie beneath the stone floors). Many give a vivid, sometimes tantalising, glimpse of their subject's life, including the one to James Bassett, who 'in the Moment of Social Pleasure, received a fall, which soon deprived him of life.'

Don't miss the one dedicated to Beau Nash ('Ricardi Nash', 'Elegantiae Arbiter', *see page 8*). Nash died at the age of 86, impoverished and enfeebled. Nonetheless his former brilliance was recalled at his death and the corporation funded a splendid funeral. Other well-known names include Sir Isaac Pitman, the inventor of shorthand, whose memorial is adorned with a winged pen, and the actor James Quin, whose epitaph was written by his friend and fellow thespian David Garrick. Quin's grave, also in the abbey, bears the inscription 'The scene is changed, I am no more/Death's the last act. Now all is o'er'. For a highly readable guide to the inscriptions, buy the pamphlet *Bath Abbey Monuments* by the rector Bernard Stace, available from the Abbey's bookshop.

James Quin memorial

21

A door on the south side of the Abbey leads to the ★ **Heritage Vaults** (Mon–Sat 10am–4pm, last admission 3.30pm, closed Sun) tracing the history of the Abbey from Saxon times to the present day. It includes an audio presentation in which well-known British actors and actresses read extracts from letters and diaries written in Bath during its Georgian heyday.

From the abbey it is a short hop to North Parade Passage and **Sally Lunn's** ❹ , a restaurant-cum museum in the oldest house in Bath (15th century, with a 17th-century facade prettified by window boxes and olde-worlde signs). Sally Lunn's is famous for a special kind of bun *(see page 67)*, which has been made on the premises since the 1680s. Its basement museum contains a 17th-century oven and archaeological finds excavated on the site.

Sally Lunn's

Route 2

The Upper Town

Queen Square – The Circus – Royal Crescent – Georgian Garden – Assembly Rooms *See map, p17*

This route is devoted to the Georgian architecture of the Upper Town, an area which became increasingly fashionable as the 18th century went on. The route takes a full day to complete, more if you want to visit all of the many museums in the area, and begins in Queen Square, a short walk northwest of the Roman Baths.

Gay Street

Quadrant of the Circus

Plane trees on Queen Square

★★ **Queen Square ❺**, built between 1729–39, was the first major undertaking of John Wood the Elder (*see page 61*) and was seminal to the development of the Palladian style in Bath. Its north side is especially striking, the Roman Portico uniting the terrace to palatial effect.

The obelisk in the centre is dedicated to Frederick Prince of Wales. It was erected by Beau Nash, in acknowledgement of a gold enamelled snuffbox which the 'King of Bath' had received from the Prince. Just north of the square, at 40 Gay Street, is the **Jane Austen Centre ❻** (Mon–Sat 10am–5.30pm, Sun 10.30am–5.30pm; admission charge) which offers a basic introduction to Austen's association with Bath. It identifies the various Bath houses in which the author lodged or lived, including No 25 Gay Street, where she stayed for a few months following her father's death.

Gay Street, named after the landowner and speculator Robert Gay with whom Wood collaborated on several building projects in the area, rises to ★★★ **The Circus ❼**, again designed by John Wood the Elder, although completed by his son. Whether inspired by the Colosseum, Stonehenge or both (a matter of conjecture), the Circus was Britain's first circular street. Note the architectural details: the acorns on the pediment, believed to allude to King Bladud (*see page 19*); the decorative frieze depicting all the arts and trades of the day; and the three types of column on the facade – Doric for the bottom storey, Ionic for the middle, and Corinthian for the top. Originally the area in the middle of the Circus, now graced by plane trees, was simply a cobbled space. Many famous people have lived on the Circus, including the statesmen William Pitt the Elder (Nos 7 and 8) and Clive of India (No 14) and the portrait painter Thomas Gainsborough (No 17).

Like his father before him, John Wood the Younger also designed an architectural first, ★★★ **The Royal Crescent ❽** (1767–74), a short walk west of the Circus, along Brock Street. The Crescent is Bath's *pièce de résistance*, not least on account of its dramatic position above Royal Victoria Park, its private lawn separated from the park by a ha-ha, giving the appearance of a seamless stretch of grass. In the latter half of the 18th century the countryside became fashionable, riding and nature rambles were introduced to the daily routine and a 'fine prospect' became desirable in homes. The meadows below the Royal Crescent formed a fashionable promenade.

No 1 Royal Crescent

Comprising 30 properties, the Crescent is astonishing in its uniformity. ★★ **No 1 Royal Crescent ❾**, the home of John Wood the Younger's father-in-law, Thomas Brock, has been turned into a museum (mid-Feb–end Oct Tues–Sun 10.30am–5pm, closed Mon except for Bank Holidays; Nov Tues–Sun 10.30am–4pm, closed Mon and Dec–mid Feb; admission charge), in which several rooms have been furnished as they might have been in the 18th century. Printed hand-outs detail items of special interest. Note the broad landing, where the sedan chairmen could turn after taking passengers to their bedroom door.

Walking along the Royal Crescent, you will encounter several plaques recalling famous past residents including Isaac Pitman (No 17), the inventor of shorthand, and Elizabeth Linley (No 11). The latter was the beautiful daughter of Thomas Linley, director of music at the Assembly Rooms. A gifted soprano, she was the darling of Bath in the 1770s, and painted by Gainsborough and Reynolds. Her engagement at the behest of her father to a wealthy but ageing suitor inspired *The Maid of Bath*, a satire by Samuel Foote. Eventually released from the unhappy betrothal, she went on to elope with the young and dashing playwright Richard Sheridan.

From the Royal Crescent **Royal Victoria Park ❿** sweeps downhill. Completed in 1830 and paid for by public subscription, the park was intended to provide space and fresh-air in the increasingly built-up city. The obelisk

23

In the Botanical Gardens and bowling in the park

Georgian Garden

Captain Wade, Master of Ceremonies from 1769–77

Chandelier in the Ball Room

on the west side of Marlborough Buildings, which dissects the park, records important episodes in the reign of Queen Victoria, who attended the opening of the park as an 11-year-old girl in 1830. While the park's eastern end offers bowling, tennis, putting, and Adventure Golf (great for kids), the dells, pool, walkways and shrubberies of the ★ **Botanical Gardens** on the western side conceal many delights – lichen-covered statues, a copy of the Temple of Minerva, a sundial, a dovecote and more. The southwest corner of the park has a superb children's play area.

At the other end of the scale from Royal Victoria Park is the ★ **Georgian Garden** ⓫ (May–Oct Mon–Fri 9am–4pm, closed weekends and Bank Holidays, free admission), off the Gravel Walk below the east side of the Royal Crescent. Excavations in 1985 to restore this walled garden to its 18th-century state revealed original paths and flowerbeds. Planted with species typical during the 1760s, it is restful in its symmetry and privacy.

Chief among the attractions of the Upper Town in Georgian times were the ★★★ **Assembly Rooms** ⓬ (daily 10am–4.30pm when not in use for private functions; last exit 5pm; admission free), in Bennett Street, on the east side of the Circus. These rooms were one of three sets in the city, the others being Harrison's (later Simpson's) and Lindsey's (later Wiltshire's) in the lower town. As the century went on there was quite a bit of rivalry between the upper and lower assemblies, and from 1777 they each had their own master of ceremonies. These Rooms, the only ones still standing, were designed by John Wood the Younger in 1769. The necessary £20,000 was raised by 'tontine' subscriptions, whereby the shares of any shareholder that died were split between remaining members. Running costs and profits were met by subscriptions: one guinea allowed up to three people to attend the season's balls, but it was necessary to take out additional subscriptions to attend concerts or to play cards.

The Rooms comprise a **ballroom**, the largest 18th-century building in Bath at 106ft (32m) long, the **Octagon**, a **Card Room** and a **Tea Room**. The ballroom is magnificent, graced by five cut-glass chandeliers. The plain area below the Corinthian columns around the wall was taken up by tiers of seating, with the front row reserved for the belles of the ball and the rear for the plain or elderly.

A ball was held once a week, beginning at 6pm with the highest ranking lady present being led onto the floor for a minuet. Minuets went on until 8pm, at which point the more energetic country dances commenced. At 9pm tea was served, followed by more dancing until 11pm. During this time non-dancers could play cards in the Octagon or, after it was added to the complex in 1777, the Card Room. Gam-

Dancing a minuet in the Tea Room

bling was one of the chief pleasures of the Georgians. Nash made his living from it, and laws curtailing gambling in 1739 and 1745 contributed to his eventual decline.

As the century wore on private parties were preferred over public balls. In 1801 Jane Austen, then living in Bath, wrote to her sister Cassandra: 'After tea we cheered up; the breaking up of private parties sent some scores more to the Ball, and tho' it was shockingly and inhumanly thin for this place, there were people enough I suppose to have made five or six very pretty Basingstoke assemblies.'

In the 19th century the Upper Rooms declined, though not without flashes of their former glory when Johann Strauss and Franz List performed and Charles Dickens gave public readings. In 1920 the rooms were converted into a cinema, and though restored by the National Trust in 1931 they were badly bombed during the Baedeker raids of 1942. Since then they have been steadily restored.

Downstairs is the ★ **Museum of Costume** (same opening times as the Assembly Rooms; admission charge). Informative guided tours lasting 30 minutes and leaving from the Octagon show how the fashions of the last five centuries have reflected their times – such as how powdered wigs suddenly went out of fashion in the 1790s when a new tax on powder was introduced to raise money for the wars with France; how sober muslins became fashionable daywear in the wake of the French Revolution when signs of wealth needed to be concealed. Though the museum covers fashion from the 16th century to the present day, the insights it gives into Georgian society are in many ways the most fascinating.

Exiting from the Assembly Rooms, turn left and then left again into **Alfred Street** where, at No 14, you can see a full complement of original Georgian ironwork framing the entrance. It includes the horn-shaped snuffers in which

25

Coat from 1894, Museum of Costume

sedan chairmen could extinguish their rag torches (links) before going inside, a boot scrape, and a winch for delivering heavy goods such as wines to the cellar. Though the ironwork is painted black, as it is all over Bath today, in the 18th century it might have been grey, green or even blue, as the Building of Bath Museum points out *(see page 27)*.

At the end of Alfred Street, a 10–15-minute walk up Lansdown Road leads to two handsome crescents, first the incomplete **Camden Crescent**, designed by John Eveleigh in 1788, and **Lansdown Crescent**, designed by John Palmer in 1789. Further north on top of Lansdown Hill (catch bus No 2 to Ensleigh and then walk a short distance north along Lansdown Road) is ★ **Beckford's Tower and Museum** (Sat & Sun and BH Mon only 10.30am–5pm, last admission 4.30pm; admission charge), which is well worth a visit if you are here on the weekend. Built in 1827 as a study-retreat for William Beckford, better known perhaps for Fonthill Abbey, his Gothic fantasy in Wiltshire, the tower offers views as far as the Forest of Dean, the Bristol Channel and Salisbury Plain from its gilded belvedere. Beckford, who inherited the estate at Fonthill plus £2 million in cash at the tender age of nine, was a flamboyant eccentric. He moved to Bath when the remodelling of Fonthill depleted his fortune and forced him to sell. The tower, which has been restored by the Bath Preservation Trust, formed the climax of a series of pleasure gardens that extended from his house in Lansdown Crescent. Beckford's tomb can be seen in the cemetery adjoining the tower.

The Countess of Huntingdon's Chapel

Back in the Upper Town, turn down Hay Hill from the end of Alfred Street to reach the Paragon. It was at No 1 the Paragon that Jane Austen stayed on her first visit to Bath in 1797. The buildings flanking the near side of the road are known as the Vineyards, on account of the vines which

The Paragon

flourished here until the land was developed in the 1760s.

A left turn here leads to the **Countess of Huntingdon's Chapel** housing the Building of Bath Museum. Selina Countess of Huntingdon (1707–91) was an aristocratic Methodist, who sold her jewels to raise money for the cause. This was the fourth chapel that she built. John Wesley preached here on a number of occasions, 'attacking the devil in his own headquarters,' as he saw it, and drew surprisingly large audiences. The presence of the Countess in Bath placed Nash in a social quandary. Though he disliked the Methodists, and had several run-ins with them, his natural snobbery inclined him to kowtow to the countess.

Museum of Bath at Work

The ★★ **Building of Bath Museum** ⓭ (Tues–Sun and BH Mon and Mon in Jul & Aug 10.30am–5pm, last admission 4.15pm; admission charge) is an illuminating account of the talents and techniques that created the lovely, seamless facades of Bath. Every aspect of building is covered, from the speculative deals that drove the building boom to the evolution of modern paints and wallpapers. Outside, a block of Bath stone invites you to test its properties with a saw.

One of the more unusual museums in the Upper Town is the ★ **Museum of Bath at Work** ⓮ (Apr–Oct daily 10.30am–4.30pm, Nov–Mar weekends only 10.30am–4.30pm; admission charge); to get there return to Lansdown Road by cutting left past the Bath Antiques Market, then take Julian Road to Christ Church). Based upon the 'Bowler Collection', the eclectic contents of a 19th-century brass foundry and soda water manufactory, the museum is a real antidote to the giddy Georgian world of baths and balls.

Jonathan Burdett Bowler was the archetypal small businessman, who built-up his engineering business through hard work and careful management. He appears to have adhered to two simple maxims: 'never throw anything away that might come in handy', and 'no job too large or small'. In 1877 he diversified into the manufacture and distribution of soda water using Bath's famous springs. The 19th-century store, engine room, workshops, office and soda factory have been reassembled here, uprooted from their original site in Corn Street in the lower town.

Exhibit in the Museum of East Asian Art

From the museum, Russell Street leads back to Bennet Street and the Assembly Rooms. As you pass Circus Place, note the **Museum of East Asian Art** ⓯ (Apr–Oct 10am–6pm, Sun 10am–5pm, Nov–Mar 10am–5pm, Sun noon–5pm; admission charge), containing an exquisite collection of Eastern antiquities acquired by lawyer Brian S. McElney during his working life in Hong Kong.

From here, Gay Street will deliver you back to where this tour began.

Route 3

Across Pulteney Bridge

Guildhall – Victoria Art Gallery – Pulteney Bridge – Great Pulteney Street – Holburne Museum – Sydney Gardens

Concentrating on the area east of the centre, this tour crosses the River Avon to Bathwick, an area free from development until Pulteney Bridge linked it to the city centre in the 1770s. It begins, however, at the Guildhall, in the High Street just behind Bath Abbey, which symbolises the growing power and wealth of the mercantile classes during the late 1700s.

Banqueting Hall

The **Guildhall** ⓰ was designed in the new Adam style *(see page 63)* in the late 1770s by Thomas Baldwin to replace an earlier building of 1625 on a different site, though the wings topped by decorative cupolas were added by John Brydon in 1891 over a century later. Baldwin was in his early twenties at the time, but his design was widely admired and he went on to become the city architect. Its ★★ **Banqueting Hall** and ante-rooms (free admission to visitors providing no functions are in progress), intended as 'assembly rooms' for the aldermen and their guests, rivalled the more exclusive Upper and Lower rooms in their magnificence. Portraits of famous Bath figures surround the large portrait of George III ('mad George') by the studio of Joshua Reynolds. Over one of the fireplaces is a portrait of Ralph Allen *(see page 29)*, by William Hoare. The chandeliers, the finest in Bath, were made in 1778 by William Parker.

Atop the Victoria Art Gallery

Next door to the Guildhall is the entrance to the **covered market** (added in 1895), a lively cut-through to the Grand Parade, and then the **Victoria Art Gallery** ⓱ (Tues–Fri 10am–5.30pm, Sat 10am–5pm, Sun 2–5pm, closed Mon; admission free) whose collection of paintings on the first floor includes Turner's *West Front of Bath Abbey*, *Adoration of the Magi*, attributed to Hugo Van der Goes, portraits by Zoffany and Gainsborough, several Sickerts and a Whistler. (Entrance to the museum is on Bridge Street.)

Bath Postal Museum

From here the High Street leads up to Northgate Street, beyond which, in Broad Street, is the **Bath Postal Museum** ⓲ (Mon–Sat 11am–5pm, closed Sun; admission charge) from where the world's first postage stamp, the Penny Black, was sent on 2 May 1840. Bath played a pivotal role in the development of the British postal system, thanks to the work of Ralph Allen, who expanded established routes and stamped out corruption, and John Palmer, who improved efficiency with the introduction of

mail coaches that were not required to stop at toll-gates. In 1784, the run from Bristol to London took just 14 hours.

Exhibits track the history of the postal service, but also touch upon some delightful peripheral topics. There is a collection of early valentines and also an 'address cabinet' of famous Bath residents, complete with portraits and biographical notes.

Back at the Victoria Art Gallery, Bridge Street leads on to ★★ **Pulteney Bridge**, first passing on the right the Grand Parade leading down to the Parade Gardens (admission charge) and thence the North and South parades (both designed by John Wood the Elder). Grand Parade (a Victorian addition) remains popular today, offering picture-postcard views of Pulteney Bridge and the weir. Though this is a recent model (1971), a weir has existed here since the Middle Ages, when it probably worked the woollen mills of the town.

Pulteney Bridge

Commissioned by William Johnstone Pulteney and designed by Robert Adam between 1770 and 1774, Pulteney Bridge, a mini Pontevechio, cost an astonishing £11,000 to build, not least on account of the tiny shops lining both sides. The bridge paved the way for the development of Bathwick (an estate owned by Pulteney), under the direction of the young Thomas Baldwin, the architect of the new Guildhall *(see page 28)*. The south side of the bridge was restored to its original glory in 1975, when outbuildings defacing its flat front were demolished; the back, however, which is visible from the Podium shopping centre or from the river, is still overhung with back kitchens and store rooms. On the right at the far end of the bridge steps lead down to the Avon, where river cruises depart for Bathampton weir every hour or so, and riverbank walks lead to North Parade Bridge (where stairs in the tollhouses offer access to the road). The tiny **Riverside Café** below Pulteney Bridge offers outside tables with views over the weir.

29

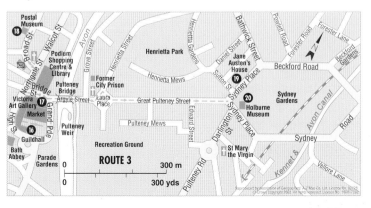

Looking down Great Pulteney Street

Jane Austen's house

Sydney Gardens

Pulteney Bridge leads into Argyle Street, off which Grove Street contains the former **City Prison**, built by Thomas Atwood in Palladian style in 1773 and now turned into flats. On the corner of Argyle and Grove streets note a *trompe l'oeil* advertising the 'George Gregory Bookshop and Lending Library' on the side of the building.

From Laura Place ★★**Great Pulteney Street** sweeps down to Sydney Gardens and the Holburne Museum. This imposing street was designed by Thomas Baldwin in the late 1780s, incorporating some elements of a previous design by Robert Adam, Pulteney's original choice of architect. The Bathwick project was interrupted by the economic slump of the 1790s and the huge array of crescents and terraces that Baldwin envisaged fanning out from Great Pulteney Street was never fully realised. Nonetheless, the street, the widest in Bath at 100ft (30m), was a fashionable address in the late 18th and early 19th centuries, as the many plaques testify. William Wilberforce (1759–1833) stayed at No 36; Emma Hamilton at No 72; Thomas Baldwin himself lived at No 6. Also here (including one in Laura Place) are two examples of the six-sided letter-boxes known as Penfold boxes, after their designer J.W. Penfold, which were used for a short while in the mid-19th century until their hexagonal design was found to trap letters.

Great Pulteney Street features in Jane Austen's *Northanger Abbey* and *Persuasion*. Austen herself lived at No 4 **Sydney Place** ⑲ between 1801 and 1804, and Queen Charlotte Sophia, consul to George III, lodged for a while at 103 Sydney Place. **Sydney Gardens** are frequently mentioned in Jane Austen's letters, as a place for public breakfasts, galas and fireworks. Later, in the 19th century, they were used for balloon ascents. Dissecting the gardens are Brunel's Great Western Railway (1840–41) and the Kennet and Avon Canal (opened 1810), industrial additions that were elegantly incorporated by means of landscaped cuttings and pretty stone and cast-iron bridges. Other attractions include a mock Roman temple.

The **Holburne Museum** ⑳, on the edge of the gardens, was originally the Sydney Hotel. The museum (mid-Feb–mid Dec Tues–Sat 10am–5pm, Sun 2.30–5.30pm, closed Mon; admission charge), based upon the collection of Sir Thomas Holburne (1793–1874), is devoted to decorative and fine art of the 17th and 18th centuries, including paintings, silver, porcelain, miniatures, glass and furniture. Among the paintings are works by Turner, Stubbs, Gainsborough and Reynolds. Gainsborough made his name in Bath, painting the portraits of the famous. His rapid success can be gauged by his escalating fees, beginning at a modest 5 guineas in 1760 and rising to 100 guineas in around 1774.

Route 4

West of the Roman Baths

**Thermae Bath Spa – St John's Hospital – Herschel
Museum – Theatre Royal – Royal Mineral Water Hospital** *See map, p17*

This route is devoted to the area west of the Roman Baths,
the site of several historic Georgian baths which form
the nucleus of Thermae Bath Spa. The tour puts special
emphasis on the city's strong medical and theatrical associations, and also pays tribute to William Herschel, an
amateur astronomer who discovered Uranus in 1781.

A few metres west of the Pump Room, along colonnaded
Bath Street (designed by Thomas Baldwin in 1791) is
★ ★ ★ **Thermae Bath Spa** ㉑ (9am–10pm, last entry
8pm; admission charge; www.thermaebathspa.com; tel:
01225 331234), a state-of-the-art spa complex that in 2003
made thermal bathing available in the city for the first time

*Bath Street Colonnade
and Cross Bath*

since the 1970s. Two-hour, four-hour and all-day mixed sex
sessions (bathing costumes must be worn; no children under 12) are available without booking, though treatments
(including hydrotherapy, hay and herbal wraps, mud treatments and shiatsu and watsu massage) must be booked. The
facilities, which include a roof-top thermal pool, incorporate two historic baths, the Cross Bath and the Hot Bath.
The pretty **Cross Bath** (Bath residents are given priority
use), which stands on its own at the end of Bath Street, is
like a giant jacuzzi inside. It has a long history of healing.
During the 17th century it had a reputation for curing sterility; Mary of Modena, the wife of James II, conceived a
much-needed heir (later the Old Pretender) after bathing
here. The current building was begun by Thomas Baldwin in 1791 and completed by John Palmer.

The **Hot Bath**, which is more obviously integrated into
the new spa complex, was built by John Wood the Younger
in 1773 in a plain, angular style. Opposite the bath, the old
Hetling Pump Room has been turned into a visitor centre,
where you can learn about the history of spa bathing in Bath
and sample the water.

Hot Baths Gallery

On the corner of Beau Street and Hot Bath Street you can
dip into the **Hot Baths Gallery** ㉒ (Mon–Sat 10am–
4.45pm, Sat 10am–4pm) to refresh your senses with contemporary art and design.

Returning to the north side of the Cross Bath, a path leads
between the buildings of the **Hospital of St John the Baptist** ㉓, founded in 1174 by Bishop Reginald Fitzjocelin.
St John's was one of several charitable hospitals built here

31

On Kingsmead Square

The Herschel Museum

during the Middle Ages, a trend begun in the 12th century by the Norman bishop John of Tours, a believer in the benefits of curative baths. Modern opinion believes many ailments were due to lead poisoning, as lead had many everyday uses at the time; it was even used as a fungicide in port wine.

Westgate Buildings lead up to Kingsmead Square, from where Avon Street, a slum area during Victorian times and heavily bombed during the Baedeker Raids of 1942, runs south through post-war development to the river. On the square is **Rosewell House** ㉔, built in 1735 by John Strahan of Bristol for Thomas Rosewell and identified by the decorative carvings festooning the central window. Though baroque architecture dominated continental cities in the 17th and early 18th centuries, this is the only baroque building in Bath.

Out on a limb at 19 New King Street (take Monmouth Street from Kingsmead Square, turn left at the end and then right), is the **Herschel Museum** ㉕ (Mar–Oct 2–5pm, Nov–Feb Sat and Sun only; admission charge), the house and observatory of William Herschel. Herschel came to Bath from Hanover in 1761 to take up a position as the organist at the Octagon Chapel on Milsom Street (now the headquarters of the Royal Photographic Society) and later succeeded Thomas Linley as musical director of the Assembly Rooms. But his abiding love was star-gazing and he would hurry home from concerts to roam through the skies with the help of home-made telescopes and his devoted sister Caroline. It was from the garden of this house that he discovered Uranus in 1781, adding to the number of known planets for the first time since antiquity. Following his discovery, Herschel was made Director of the Royal Astronomical Observatory. The museum documents Herschel's two careers. In the basement is the workshop where he built his telescopes.

Return towards the city centre via Monmouth Street, at the end of which Saw Close runs up to the **Theatre Royal** ㉖, the hub of Bath's thriving theatre scene from 1805, when the hitherto renowned Orchard Street Theatre moved here. Orchard Street was associated with some of the finest actors of the day, including James Quin, David Garrick and Sarah Siddons. The city also drew dramatists who set their plays in Bath – invariably farces pivoting on the collision of town and country manners. Richard Sheridan joined his family in Bath in 1771, but made his name in London with *The Rivals*, a satire set in Bath (which his friend Frederick Reynolds mocked in *The Dramatist*, also set in Bath). In Bath, Sheridan was famous for eloping with Elizabeth Linley, daughter of Thomas Linley and

Theatre Royal interior

the inspiration for Samuel Foote's play *The Maid of Bath*. It is worth trying to see a performance at the theatre; the entrance on Saw Close leads to swagged and gilded tiers of plush red velvet seating.

Derek Jacobi's hands

In **Seven Dials**, the small square, behind the theatre, the handprints of British actors and actresses, including John Gielgud, Michael Hordern and Derek Jacobi are cast in bronze around the former fountain.

Next to the theatre is the house (now Popjoy's restaurant) in which Beau Nash died in 1761, tended by his mistress Juliana Papjoy. He lived here, next door to the home he occupied during the height of his success, for the last 16 years of his life, surviving on a pension of just £10 a month.

From here, Barton Street leads up to Queen Square, the start of Route 2 (*see page 22*), but turn right along Upper Borough Walls to reach the Royal Mineral Water Hospital. On the way is a view of St John's Gate (also called Trim Bridge) spanning Queen Street. **The Royal Mineral Water Hospital ㉗** was a philanthropic venture built on the site of a theatre by John Wood the Elder between 1738 and 1742, under the collective auspices of Dr William Oliver of Bath Oliver biscuit fame, Ralph Allen, who provided the stone, and Beau Nash, who raised funds for the project. Ongoing expenses were met by fines levied on illegal gambling and by collections at church services. The hospital is still in use as the Royal National Hospital for Rheumatic Diseases.

33

Directly in front of the hospital Old Bond Street leads up to Milsom Street, which was laid out in the 1760s. Among its chic shops is the **Octagon Chapel**, now the headquarters for the Royal Photographic Society, which was designed by Thomas Lightholer in 1767 as a propietary (subscription) chapel with fireplaces, carpets and 'every accommodation of ease and refinement'. Union Street, also good for shopping, leads back to Stall Street and the Pump Room, where this route began.

Milsom Street

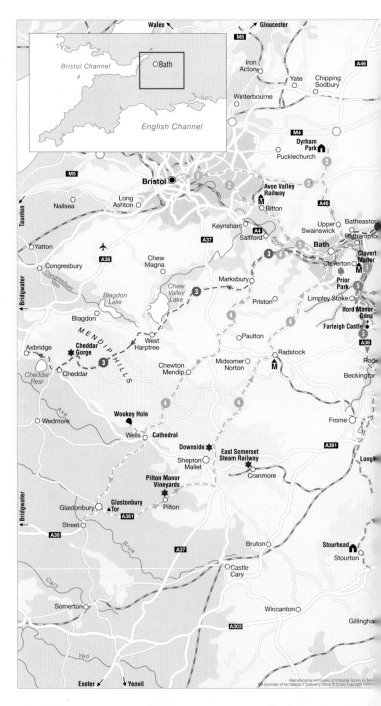

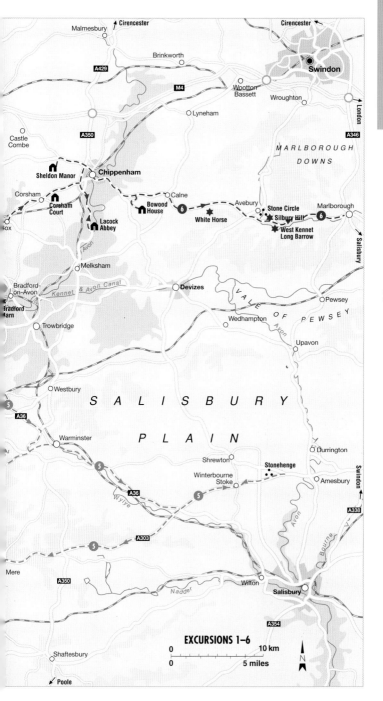

Malmesbury

↑ Cirencester

Cirencester ←

Brinkworth

A429

Swindon

M4

Wootton
Bassett

Wroughton

A350

Lyneham

London

Castle
Combe

MARLBOROUGH

DOWNS

A346

Sheldon Manor

Chippenham

Corsham

Calne

Avebury

Stone Circle

Marlborough

Corsham
Court

Bowood
House

6

White Horse

Silbury Hill

ox

Lacock
Abbey

West Kennet
Long Barrow

6

Salisbury

Avon

Melksham

Bradford-
on-Avon

Kennet & Avon Canal

Devizes

VALE

Pewsey

Bradford
Barn

Trowbridge

Wedhampton

OF

PEWSEY

Avon

Upavon

Westbury

S   A   L   I   S   B   U   R   Y

5

A36

Warminster

P   L   A   I   N

Durrington

5

Shrewton

Stonehenge

Swindon

A36

Winterbourne
Stoke

5

Amesbury

Wylye

A338

5

A303

Avon

Bourne

Mere

A350

Nadder

Wilton

Salisbury

A354

EXCURSIONS 1–6

0   10 km

0   5 miles

N

Shaftesbury

↙ Poole

Excursion 1

Bradford-on-Avon

American Museum – Bradford-on-Avon – Iford Manor Gradens – Farleigh Hungerford Castle *See map, p34–5*

Local face in Bradford-on-Avon

The former mill town of **Bradford-on-Avon** lies just 8 miles (13km) from Bath). It offers a picturesque riverside location, a rich industrial heritage, one of the best Saxon churches in the country and a 14th-century tithe barn. Though the distance is short, the route described here, which also takes in the highly recommended American Museum and Iford Manor Gardens, is likely to take a full day to complete. It is designed with car drivers in mind, but both the American Museum and Bradford-on-Avon are easily reached by public transport: for the museum, take bus No 18 to Bath University (plus a 10-minute walk), and for Bradford-on-Avon Nos X4, X5 or X6, departing from the bus station. Drivers should leave Bath on the A36 bypassing Bathampton (home and burial place of Sickert, two of whose paintings are in the Victoria Art Gallery in Bath), turning right for the American Museum (signposted) after 3 miles (5km).

Occupying neoclassical Claverton Manor (1820) on Claverton Down, the ★★ **American Museum** (last week Mar–end Oct/beginning Nov: Tues–Thur garden 1–6pm, museum 2–5pm, Fri–Sun garden noon–6pm, museum 2–5pm, closed Mon except during Aug and Bank Holidays; also last week Nov–mid-Dec 1–4pm, plus Wed evening 5.30–7.30pm, closed Mon; www.americanmuseum.org) offers an absorbing picture of American domestic life between the 17th and 19th centuries. The attention to detail and the informative staff make this one of the best museums in the region.

Claverton Manor

A series of rooms have been furnished according to various eras and areas, a number of them shipped from the USA and reassembled. There are some 12 interiors altogether (plus smaller reconstructions), ranging from the 17th-century Keeping Room to the elegant 18th-century 'Deer Park Parlour' from Maryland, the Stencilled Bedchamber (c1830), and the 'Greek Revival Room', based on a New York dining room c1824–35. The New Orleans Bedroom, with its blood-red wall-paper, ornate Louis XV-style half-tester bed, dressing table and love seat, evokes the ante-bellum world of the young Scarlett O'Hara. In addition, there are displays documenting westward expansion, whaling, the history of the North American Indian, and American arts and crafts such as quilting, Indian beading and Shaker furniture-making. In Conkey's Tav-

Just like Mount Vernon

ern visitors can warm themselves by a real fire and sample home-made sticky gingerbread.

The American theme extends to the manor's grounds, with a replica of George Washington's rose and flower garden at Mount Vernon, complete with a copy of the garden house that served as a school for the president's step-grandchildren; a colonial herb garden; a teepee; and a 'milliner's shop', containing a collection of decorated bandboxes. A gallery of American Folk Art occupies the former stables; visit the tea-room for real American cookies.

Leaving the American Museum, turn right at the A36 and then, just before Limpley Stoke, left along the B3108 to ★★ **Bradford-on-Avon**.

The history of this scenic town on the Avon is rooted in the woollen industry, which flourished in the region during the late Middle Ages, evolving from a simple trade in wool to a cottage-based weaving industry. By the 18th century it was factory based with specialised machinery, but by then the industry was already in decline, squeezed by competition from towns in northern England, such as Bradford in Yorkshire.

37

Evidence of the wool and cloth industry are everywhere in Bradford: weavers' cottages, the mills flanking the river, and the decorated merchants' houses. The town also has a large number of non-conformist chapels. John Wesley preached here and the tireless Countess of Huntingdon (*see page 26*) was active.

The focal point of the town is the main **bridge** (a 17th-century remodelling of a 13th-century original), crossing the 'broad ford' which gives the town its name and offering a picture-postcard view of the town piled upon the hill behind. In the middle of the bridge is a 'chapel' – actually a 17th-century lock-up for miscreants, though

Georgian townhouses and the Bridge

Bridge Tea Rooms and interior of the Saxon church

the 13th-century bridge may have included a chapel for pilgrims on their way to Glastonbury.

Off Market Street, Church Street leads to the Saxon ★ **church of St Laurence**, founded by St Adhelm in around 700 but rebuilt in 1001, with carved angels over the chancel arch. St Laurence was recovered from secular use (part school from 1715, and part cottage) in around 1871, 15 years after the vicar, an amateur archaeologist, discovered the two carved angels. Close to St Laurence is the Norman parish church.

Back on Market Street, the Shambles, the site of the town's medieval market, leads off to the right, and at the top of the street is Priory Barn belonging to the manor from which the porch in the garden at Corsham Court (*see page 55*) originally belonged. The Methuen family of Corsham were leading players in the wool industry in Bradford; a memorial to Thomas Methuen (1684–1733) can be found in the parish church here, along with other memorials to Bradford cloth merchants.

Signposted off the Frome road on the edge of town is the ★ **Bradford Barn**, an early 14th-century tithe barn. Tithes, a 'tenth' of the agricultural produce of a parish which was paid as a tax to the Church, were first introduced by King Offa of Mercia in the 8th century. This particular barn would also have been used for storing the produce of the Abbess of Shaftesbury's estate, to which Bradford belonged.

From here, a gentle walk of about 2 miles (3km) along the towpath of the Kennet and Avon canal leads to the pretty village of **Avoncliff**. Alternatively, bikes can be hired by the day, half-day or hour from Lock Inn Cottage, off the Frome road (*see page 71*).

Leaving Bradford by the Frome road (the B3109), you can visit the Italianate **Iford Manor Gardens** (Apr and Oct, Sun and Easter 2–5pm; May–Sept 2–5pm, closed Mon and Fri; admission charge; free for children under 10 years of age but children are not admitted at the weekend). Designed by the Edwardian architect and gardener Harold Peto (1899–1933), who once lived here, it is a tranquil and romantic spot offering outstanding rural views.

The exit from the gardens leads to the A36, where a right turn will deliver you back to Bath. Alternatively, a left turn leads to the junction with the A366 to Trowbridge, off which is **Farleigh Hungerford Castle** (English Heritage) converted into a castle from a medieval manor house by Sir Thomas Hungerford in the late 14th century (Apr–Sept 10am–6pm, Oct 10am–5pm, Nov–Mar Wed–Sun 10am–1pm and 2–4pm; admission charge). The ruins include the two south towers, the curtain wall, the gatehouse and the chapel. Picnics are permitted in the grounds.

Iford Manor Gardens

38

Excursion 2

Bristol

Bristol – Dyrham Park *See map, p34–5*

While Bath is primarily a city of pleasure, Bristol, 13 miles (21km) away, is a city of industry. A major British port for 300 years, second only to London, Bristol was – and still is to a lesser extent – the West Country's window on the world and its main magnet for labour. But Bristol's industrial character doesn't mean it has nothing to interest visitors. Important since Saxon times – and a port of call for Phoenician traders long before that – it has a rich history plus an attractive setting afforded by the cliffs of the Avon. With seagulls wheeling overhead and salty breezes off the Bristol Channel, the city makes an invigorating change from cosy, compact Bath.

Bristol Temple Meads

39

There are two direct roads to Bristol from Bath, the A4 and the A431 (the latter passing **Avon Valley Railway** steam train museum at Bitton). Buses to Bristol (journey time around 45 minutes) leave from Bath Bus Station every 15 minutes (Bristol Bus Station is located behind Broadmead Shopping Centre, from where you should follow signposts to The Centre Promenade). Alternatively, regular trains leave from Bath Spa to Bristol Temple Meads (journey time 15–30 minutes, depending on train).

A stone's throw from Bristol Temple Meads Station, and occupying Old Bristol Station, designed by Isambard Kingdom Brunel, is the superb ★★★ **British Empire & Commonwealth Museum** (10am–5pm; admission charge; www.empire museum.co.uk), charting Britain's colonial expansion from 1500 until its peak in 1914, when Britain

Clifton Suspension Bridge

ruled more than a quarter of the world, and then its relatively rapid decline and fall. Located in Bristol because of the city's role as a gateway to the empire and also as a hub for the slave industry, the museum pulls no punches. However, there is lots of fun to be had here too, especially for children, with plenty of hands-on displays and interesting temporary exhibitions, such as On Your Marks, inviting children to test their skills at sports from around the world.

From the museum, you can follow signposts to the Harbourside (a 15–20-minute walk, or bus Nos 8 or 9), the focus of a cluster of attractions and museums that have flowered in the redeveloped docks, including the **Arnolfini Arts Centre** (closed until completion of a major redevelopment in 2005) and ★ ★ **At-Bristol** (10am–6pm; admission charge; www.at-bristol.org.uk). The latter is a child-oriented, hands-on heaven comprising Wildwalk@Bristol, in which a lush bird- and butterfly-inhabited 'rainforest' is interspersed with interactive displays, Explore@Bristol, a state-of-the-art science centre, and an IMAX cinema.

The Watershed

Just outside At-Bristol, you'll find Bristol's **Tourist Information Centre** (Mar–Oct 10am–6pm, Nov–Feb Mon–Sat 10am–5pm, Sun 11am–4pm).

There are numerous cafés, bars and restaurants in this area, particularly along the **Watershed**, a finger of the Floating Harbour, created in 1810 as a non-tidal dock and now one of the most vibrant areas in this distinctly party city. From below Neptune's statue on the Watershed ferries leave for the *SS Great Britain* and to other landing stages every 40 minutes or so. Alternatively, the ship can be reached by walking along Narrow Quay, past the Arnolfini Arts Complex, and across Prince Street Bridge, where a right turn leads along the south side of the Floating Harbour).

SS Great Britain

★ *SS Great Britain* (Apr–Oct 10am–5.30pm, Nov–Mar 10am–4.30pm) represents Bristol's heyday as a major shipbuilding centre, when the city inspired the expression 'ship-shape and Bristol fashion'. First floated in 1843, it was the first propeller-driven iron ocean-going ship in history and was intended to wipe out the lead that America had gained in transatlantic passenger shipping in the previous 30 years. Designed by Isambard Kingdom Brunel, chief engineer of the Great Western Steamship Company, the vessel measured 322ft (98m) in length, had a gross tonnage of 2,936, and was fitted with six masts, for use when the wind was favourable in order to save coal. As well as surpassing other ships in terms of speed and capacity, it set new standards of comfort.

But in 1946, the year after its first voyage, the captain grounded the ship in Dundrum Bay off Ireland. The cost of repairs and repeated attempts at refloating bankrupted the Great Western Steamship Company and the ship was bought by Gibbs, Bright and Company of Liverpool. It was substantially altered for its relaunch in 1852, after which it spent 24 years transporting emigrants to Australia. It is estimated that some 250,000 Australians are descended from its passengers. Near the *SS Great Britain* is *The Matthew* (10am–5.30pm; admission charge), a reconstruction of the ship in which John Cabot set sail for America in 1497 under patent of Henry VII. Cruises aboard *The Matthew* are offered on Tuesday and Thursday evenings (tel: 0117 922 0441).

Also here is the **Maritime Heritage Museum** (same hours as *SS Great Britain*), detailing Bristol's history as a port and shipbuilding centre. The 20th century brought decline for the shipbuilding industry, and by the 1920s there was only one commercial shipyard left in Bristol.

Along the waterfront

Return along the quay to the ★ **Industrial Museum** (Apr–Oct Sat–Wed 10am–5pm, closed Thur and Fri; Nov–Mar weekends only 10am–5pm; admission charge), a vast hangar-type structure with Bristol's shipping and aero-engine industries represented upstairs and the history of transport downstairs. Exhibits range from a cross-section of Concorde (produced in Bristol in 1969) to the accounts of an 18th-century slave ship.

41

Inside the Industrial Museum

Back at the Watershed, Park Street leads uphill to the city centre and the university. Half-way up on the left are College Green and ★★ **Bristol Cathedral**, originally the church of an Augustinian abbey founded in around 1140 by Robert Fitzardinge. The abbey was closed following the dissolution of the monasteries in 1539 but the church was reopened as a cathedral in 1542. It is a rare example of a hall church, in which the roof is at the same height throughout the building. This makes it extremely strong. Though Bristol was heavily bombed during World War II, the cathedral escaped relatively lightly.

This tour of the interior leads in a clockwise direction. The original unfinished **nave** was demolished after the dissolution, resulting in a truncated church right up until the mid-19th century. This nave was added in 1868–77 by George Edmund Street. At the **crossing**, an upward glance to the right will alight on variously decorated bosses in the vaulting of the south transept, added in the 15th century.

The **Elder Lady Chapel** (1220) contains some fine naturalistic carvings of animals, including monkeys, linking it to the stone mason who worked on Wells cathedral, where similar carvings are found *(see page 47)*.

The **choir** (1298–1330) has lierne-rib vaulting, the ear-

Elder Lady Chapel

Eastern Lady Chapel

liest of its kind in England. The choir stalls have finely carved misericords (ledges on the underside of the hinged seats, designed to prop up the choristers).

The **Eastern Lady Chapel** (1298), behind the High Altar, is interesting for its deep green, blue, red and gold paintwork (partially restored in 1935); medieval cathedrals would have been covered in such colours. The heraldry on the screen and around the edge of the east window relates to the Berkeley family, descendants of the founder of the abbey, to whom this chapel was originally dedicated. The parapet was given by one of the last abbots, Abbot Burton (1526–30), who is represented by a rebus (visual pun): a thistle (for Bur) and a barrel (for ton).

As you turn into the south aisle, a doorway leads into the sacristy and **Berkeley Chapel**, the former containing windows filled with fragments of early stained glass and framed by charming stone carvings of foliage, including a snail. In the left-hand niche of the sacristy is a flue for the oven in which bread for the Eucharist was baked.

Further up the south aisle is a chapel to the Newton family. Past here is the entrance to the Chapter House and Cloisters. As you turn towards these, note, on the left, the Saxon stone sculpture (c.1050) depicting the *Harrowing of Hell* (a just discernible Christ trampling Satan while comforting a pregnant woman), one of the most important pieces of Saxon sculpture in England. The Norman **Chapter House** (1150) was the scene of social unrest in 1831, when rioters threatened to burn down the cathedral.

From the cathedral, Park Street rises to Bristol University and the City Museum and Art Gallery, passing on the left Great George Street containing the late 18th-century ★ **Georgian House** (Sat–Wed 10am–5pm; admission charge), said to be where Wordsworth first met Coleridge in 1795. It was a Bristol company, Biggs and Cottle that first printed their *Lyrical Ballads* (1798). Off to the right at the top of Park Street is Park Row, containing the **Red Lodge** (Apr–Oct Sat–Wed 10am–5pm; admission charge), a Tudor lodge with fine woodwork.

A left turn at the top of Park Street leads into Queen's Road which runs up to **Clifton Village** (also accessed by buses Nos 8 and 9 from College Green outside the cathedral) where Isambard Kingdom Brunel's ★★**Suspension Bridge** (1829–1864) spans the gorge. A Visitor Centre (summer 10am–5pm; winter 11am–4pm, until 5pm on weekends; admission charge) relates the story behind the building of the bridge. Though Brunel won the commission at the age of 24, he never saw the finished bridge, as he died five years before its completion. Close to the bridge is **Clifton Observatory** (summer 11am–5pm, winter noon–4pm; admission charge), offering a camera obscura.

Isambard Kingdom Brunel

After visiting the bridge, you may want to wander around **Clifton Village**, whose Georgian buildings are occupied by interesting shops, cosy restaurants and cafés, or visit the nearby **Bristol Zoological Gardens** (daily 9am–5.30pm, until 4.30pm in winter; admission charge.

Further sights

★ **St Mary Redcliffe**, passed on the footpath to Bristol Temple Meads station, was built between 1325–75 in the Perpendicular style, the last stage of English Gothic architecture characterised by pinnacles and projecting buttresses. Its soaring spire is 285-ft (87-m) tall. Interesting features of the church include the hexagonal 13th-century north porch with an inner 12th-century porch, fan vaulting and aisled transepts. Famous figures associated with the church are the poets Thomas Chatterton (1752–70), who lived nearby, and Southey and Coleridge who were married to two sisters by the name of Fricker here in 1795.

St Mary Redcliffe

Also worth seeing are two monuments to the Methodist Movement, which was particularly strong in the West Country: ★ **Wesley's New Room** (36 Horsefair, near Broadmead Shopping Centre; 10am–1pm and 2–4pm), an engaging museum to Wesley and the Methodist movement, and **Charles Wesley's House** (open by appointment for groups, tel: 0117 926 4740), the home of John Wesley's famous hymn-writing brother.

To take in ★★ **Dyrham Park** (National Trust; house: Apr–Oct noon–5pm, closed Wed &Thur; grounds: year-round 11am–5.30pm), 12 miles/19km from Bristol) leave Bristol by the A420, turning left at the junction with the A46 (special buses to Dyrham also depart from Bath Bus Station). Though built on the bones of a Tudor manor, the current house dates from 1692–1704 when William Blathwayt, Secretary of State to William III, remodelled it in baroque style. There have been few changes to the house since, but the grounds were altered in around 1800 when improvements in the Bath-Gloucester road made an east entrance to the house more convenient than the existing west one. The formal gardens were moved to the east and the steeply rising hills, previously covered in terraces and walks, were turned into parkland. The work was carried out by Charles Harcourt-Masters with input from landscape architect Humphry Repton. Only the staircase cascade of 224 steps in the spur of the hills remains of the previous design. The deer park, however, has existed here for centuries (*deor hamm* being Anglo-Saxon for deer enclosure).

Dyrham Park

Inside, the house incorporates a variety of Dutch and Flemish features reflecting William Blathwayt's diplomatic connections with Holland. From Dyrham the A46 winds down Swainswick hill to Bath (8 miles/13km).

Excursion 3

The Mendip Hills

Prior Park – Chew Valley Lake – Cheddar Gorge *See map, p34–5*

This tour heads southwest of Bath to Cheddar Gorge in the Mendip Hills, one of southern England's most famous beauty spots and the home of its most popular cheese. Though now a rather gaudy shrine to West Country pastoralism, Cheddar offers lovely walks and has lots of attractions for children. If you have time, this route links up well with Excursion 4 to Wells Cathedral.

Chew Valley Lake

From Bath take the A36 Lower Bristol Road, passing on the left, after crossing the Kennet and Avon Canal, Prior Park Road (A3062) leading to the former village of Widcombe and **Prior Park**. This is now a school but the grounds are owned by the National Trust (Feb–Nov 11am–5.30pm, closed Tues; Dec–Jan Fri–Sun only 11am–dusk; admission charge). As there is no parking close by, you may find it best to visit Prior Park on another day, taking bus Nos 2 or 4 from Bath Bus Station. The country home of Ralph Allen *(see page 8)*, the mansion was built by John Wood the Elder between 1734 and 1742 close to Allen's stone quarries at Combe Down. With its imposing portico, this is rated as one of the finest Palladian buildings in Britain. It was here that Allen held open house to the leading statesmen, writers and artists of the day, such as William Pitt, Alexander Pope, Henry Fielding and Gainsborough; indeed, the munificent Squire Allworthy in Fielding's *Tom Jones* was based on Allen. The delightful walk through the grounds takes in lovely views of Bath and also a lake crossed by a Palladian bridge reminiscent of the one at Stowe.

The Lower Bristol Road is an industrial exit from Bath, running parallel with the railway line before joining the A4. Around 3 miles (5km) from Bath, take the A39 Wells road, then at Marksbury take the A368. At 15 miles (24km) from Bath, the road crosses the southern tip of ★ **Chew Valley Lake**, a reservoir created in 1956 that draws fly fishermen, sailors and birdlife. It has one of the largest reed beds in southwest England, inhabited by over 260 species of birds, including shovelers, gadwell, teal and the great crested grebe, and is skirted by meadows and woodland rich in butterflies, dragonflies and flora. Special trails (the Bittern Trail, the Grebe Trail), punctuated by hides, lead around the eastern shores . For details on fishing at Chew (and neighbouring Blagdon), *see page 71*.

Follow the A368 through West Harptree and then follow signposts to join the B3371 to Cheddar (25 miles/ 40km from Bath), passing en route the turning for Charterhouse, a centre for Roman lead mining and source of the lead sheets lining the Great Bath at Bath.

★★ **Cheddar Gorge**, the biggest gorge (3 miles/5km long) in Britain, was carved out of the karst limestone by the Yeo River. Much of the land is part of the Marquess of Bath's **Cheddar Caves and Gorge** (daily 10.30am–4.30pm; admission charge), though the north side of the gorge is in the hands of the National Trust, and public footpaths crisscross the whole of the gorge. A range of entertainments have sprung up for tourists, who have been coming here in droves ever since the railway to Bristol opened in 1869. The chief attractions are the show-caves, which are the most spectacular in the many caves and swallowholes that burrow through the Mendip Hills.

★ **Gough's Caves**, carved out by the meltwaters of the last Ice Age and inhabited from the Stone Age, were discovered by Richard Gough in 1890 and opened to the public in 1898. It was here that the skeleton of the 9,000-year-old Cheddar Man was discovered in 1903. A walkway leads through a series of chambers encrusted with stalactites, the colours of which range through grey (lead), red (iron oxide), green (copper carbonate) and white (calcium). The formations grow at the rate of approximately one cubic inch every thousand years.

The admission charge to Gough's Cave also includes entrance to ★ **Cox's Cave** (discovered 1836), where the Crystal Quest presents a subterranean battle between good and evil, in which princesses and wizards prevail and dragons and goblins are defeated. Children love it, and even adults emerge smiling. Cox's Cave exits at **Jacob's Ladder**, a flight of 237 steps, each representing 1 million years in the history of our planet (the history of man is equivalent to a piece of writing paper placed on the top step). Above the gorge, **Pavey's Tower** offers views over the Mendips and beyond. A pretty walk leads for 5 miles (8km) around the top of the gorge.

Further down Cliff Road, the main street of Cheddar is packed with tea-rooms, glass-blowers, fudge-makers, cider barns and cheese shops. All of these come under one roof at **The Cheddar Gorge Cheese Co** (mid-Mar–Apr daily 10am–4pm, May –30 Sept daily 10am–6pm) with a working dairy documenting the history of cheese-making in Cheddar over the last 700 years. The dairy is augmented by a cooperage, spinner and potter.

From Cheddar the A371 leads west to Axbrige, the site of the National Trust's **King John's Hunting Lodge** (Apr–Sept daily 1–4pm; admission free), a late medieval merchant's house. In the other direction, the A371 leads east to Wells (11 miles/17km) (*see Excursion 4*).

Cheddar Gorge

Gough's Caves

Cheddar Gorge Cheese Co

Excursion 4

To Wells

Bath – Wells – Wookey Hole Caves – Glastonbury – Shepton Mallet *See map, p34–5*

In spite of the many stately homes, areas of outstanding natural beauty and tourist attractions surrounding Bath, for many people Wells Cathedral is the one compelling reason for venturing out of the city.

The A367 Wells road is clearly signposted from the south of Bath (like Excursion 3, it passes the road to Prior Park, *see page 44*). Around 10 miles (16 km) south of Bath are the market towns of Midsomer Norton and Radstock. In Midsomer Norton, the River Somer runs alongside the main street, making it an attractive place in which to stop for a coffee and browse in the characterful town centre.

From here, the route crosses to the A39, for the descent into Wells. Two miles (3km) off to the righ just outside Wells are ★**Wookey Hole Caves** (summer daily 10am–5pm and winter daily 10.30am–4.30pm, closed for a week at Christmas; admission charge) where guided tours explore caves carved out by the River Axe, which rises to the surface inside the caves. In competition with Cheddar, Wookey Hole offers other entertainments, mainly aimed at children, including an Edwardian fairground, a mirror maze, tours of the 19th-century paper mil, and demonstrations of paper-making by hand.

Wookey Hole Caves

Wells (population: 9,000), 23 miles (37km) from Bath, is a sleepy market town lifted completely out of the ordinary by its stunning ★★★ **Cathedral Church of St Andrew** and **Bishop's Palace**. Like Bath, it derives its name from natural springs which were probably associated with a pre-Christian shrine. In 705 a church was founded by Aldhelm, Bishop of Sherborne. The Diocese of Wells was created in 909, though the see was moved to Bath by John of Tours in around 1088. It returned to Wells under Bishop Savaric (1192), but in 1244 was split between the two cities with the creation of the Diocese of Bath and Wells.

The Cathedral that you see today was begun in 1179 and completed in 1340. It is in the Early English Gothic style, characterised by pointed arches and ribbed vaulting. Unlike Bath Abbey, it was a cathedral rather than a monastery and survived the Dissolution intact, though it suffered repeated damage during the Civil War and Monmouth's Rebellion in the 17th century.

Parking is available either in the market place. From

Market day in Wells

here the **Penniless Porch** – still used by beggars today – leads to the intricately carved **West Front** incorporating 293 statues of angels, kings, knights, bishops and saints (13th century) rising to a central band of 12 apostles (15th century) and the figure of Christ in Majesty at its apex, carved in 1985 by David Wynne to replace the crumbling original. Erosion and destruction by puritans in the 17th century have left many of the lower niches vacant, but the front remains a breathtaking sight, its unusual breadth due to the towers being placed either side of the nave instead of head on. Originally the statues would have numbered around 400 and been richly painted in bright colours.

Inside the cathedral, the eye is swept along the nave to the great scissor-arches at the transept, pulled by the succession of arches and the vaulted ceiling, the delicate decoration of which was discovered under whitewash in the 19th century. In the Middle Ages the only seating in the cathedral would have been stone benches running around the sides of the naves and their aisles.

Pinnacle of the West Front

An anti-clockwise walk around the cathedral:

A **Sugar Chantry** (1489). Commemorates Hugh Sugar, the cathedral's treasurer. Chantries were built by wealthy members of the congregation so that masses might be offered in their memory after death.

B **The Font**. The base was brought from the old Saxon cathedral (on the site of the cloisters); the exquisite 17th-century cover was painted and gilded in 1982. Carvings on the pillars near the font depict scenes from everyday life in the Middle Ages: a man taking a thorn out of his foot, a cobbler at work, a man nursing a toothache. The scenes decorating one pillar, carved in around 1190, tells the complete story

47

Wells Cathedral

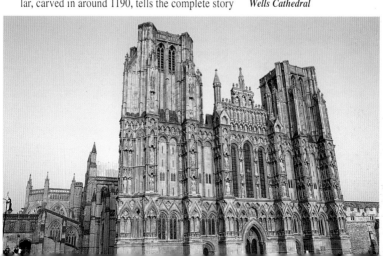

Choir and Jesse window

of a man and a boy stealing fruit from an orchard and being caught, chased and punished by the farmer.

C **Memorial Chapel to St Calixtus**

D **Memorial Chapel to St Martin**

E ★★★ **The Choir**. This is the heart of the cathedral. On the underside of the seats are finely carved misericords (to support the clerics during periods in the service when they are required to stand). The east window (1340) depicts the lineage of Christ, with Jesse, King David (son of Jesse) and Mary. It is one of the oldest Jesse windows in Britain. High up above the choir are small niches where boy sopranos would have played the part of angels on feast days.

F **South Choir Aisle**. A number of important tombs are found here: on the left (moving east), the Tomb of Bishop Harewell (1380), with its rebus (visual pun) on his name in the carving; the effigies of three Saxon Bishops, whose bones were transferred here from the Saxon cathedral in around 1200, when Wells was trying to regain cathedral status for the church of St Andrew; and the good Bishop Bekynton's tomb, with its grim reminder of death (the bishop's corpse rotting in his shroud) on the bottom rung. Beckington, Bishop of Bath and Wells between 1443–65 built the choir school over the West Cloister, the Chain Bridge and, for the people of Wells, a row of 12 houses in the marketplace. At the eastern end of the aisle are three examples of carved misericords (*see* E).

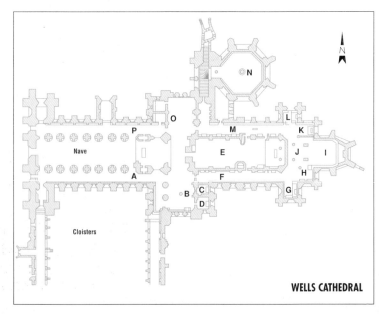

WELLS CATHEDRAL

G **St Catherine's Chapel**. The stained glass here was salvaged from a church in Rouen (desecrated during the French Revolution) in 1813.

H **St John the Baptist Chapel**

I ★★ **Lady Chapel**. Built in 1326, originally as a separate building. The Lady Chapel windows were shattered during the Civil War (1642–7) and Monmouth's Protestant Rebellion (1685). Only the upper sections contain the original glass. The brass lectern at the entrance to the Lady Chapel was given by Dean Robert Creyghton to mark the restoration of King Charles II in 1660.

J **Retrochoir**. Built to unite the Lady Chapel with the presbytery. The ribs in the lovely vaulting were decorated by T H Willement in 1845. Notice the magnificent 13th-century cope (cloak) chest nearby.

K **St Stephen's Chapel**

L **Chapel of Corpus Christi**. Reserved for private prayer.

M **North Choir Aisle**. Among the tombs are that of Bishop Giso (d.1088), brought here from the Saxon cathedral, and the alabaster tomb of Bishop Ralph of Shrewsbury (d. 1363), who founded the College of Vicars and built the Vicars' Hall.

49

Stairs to and ceiling of the Chapter House

N ★★★ **The Chapter House**. The curving flight of steps leading up to the octagonal Chapter House was built in the 13th century. Worn by age and use, the lovely honey-coloured stone is illuminated by windows containing the oldest stained glass in the cathedral. The Chapter House itself, where cathedral business was carried out (and still is today on important occasions), was completed in 1306. Seating for 49 canons line the walls, each space marked by the name of the estate; above, 32 tiercorn ribs (precursor of fan vaulting) spray from a central pier. As you leave the Chapter House, a narrow flight of stairs (added in 1459) leads off to the Chain Bridge which links the cathedral with the Vicar's Hall.

O ★★★ **Clock**. This medieval clock is one of the treasures of the cathedral. It actually has two faces: one on the exterior wall of the cathedral, the other here. Still keeping time today (though the original internal mechanism is in the Science Museum in London) it comprises three dials, the outer one indicating the hours on a 24-hour clockface, the middle one showing the minutes, and the inner one marking the date of the lunar month. Try to catch the clock striking the hour, when jousting knights rotate.

This is also the best place to view the beautiful ★★★ **scissor arches**, added by master mason William Joy between 1338–48. Though built to solve tech-

Scissor arches

nical problems – the weight of the tower, enlarged by Dean John Godelee in 1313, was straining the foundations – the visual effect is stunning.

P   Bubwith's Chantry. In honour of Bishop Bubwith.

Cloister restaurant

The **Cloisters**, partly occupied by the cathedral shop and restaurant, are approached from the southwest side of the nave. Replacing the smaller 13th-century cloisters, they were completed in 1508. Above the East Cloister is the medieval library, financed by a legacy of Bishop Bubwith (d.1424), containing around 6,000 books. A door in the south cloister leads to the Bishop's Palace (also accessible from Market Place).

Bishop's Palace

The ★★ **Bishop's Palace and Gardens** (Easter Sat–end of Oct, Tues–Fri & Bank Holiday Mon 10.30am–6pm, Sun 1–6pm; plus occasional opening on Monday and Saturday, tel: 01749 678691 for details; admission charge) was begun in the early 13th century by Bishop Jocelin and enlarged by successive bishops until the mid-15th century. Moated and approached over a drawbridge, it was clearly designed for defence. Such features were added by Bishop Ralph of Shrewsbury in the 14th century.

The **Henderson Rooms** form the oldest part of the palace. In the First Floor Hall style, they comprise a ground-floor cellar from which a Jacobean staircase installed by Bishop Montague (1608–16) leads to a suite of state rooms: the **Long Gallery**, lined with portraits of past bishops, many of whom played key roles in English history; a Victorian-style **Drawing Room**, overlooking Bishop Jocelin's deer park (now pasture); the **Conference Room**, with its elaborate plaster ceiling and carpet from Windsor Castle; and **Panelled Room**, in which portraits of more recent bishops are displayed. Also open to visitors is the adjoining **Bishop's Chapel**, the private chapel of the Bishop of Bath and Wells.

In the tranquil grounds of the palace are the springs which gave Wells its name. They were harnessed by Bishop Beckynton in the 15th century to supply the palace with water and to drive the town's woollen mills. As you

Great Hall ruins

make your way back to the gatehouse, note the ruins of the **Great Hall**, built by Bishop Robert Burnell (1275–93). During the Reformation, the hall was the scene of the trial of the abbot and treasurer of Glastonbury Abbey, accused of sedition for their opposition to Henry VIII's severance from the Church of Rome. Found guilty, they were executed on Glastonbury Tor (*see page 51*).

From the gatehouse, a pleasant walk off to the left skirts the grounds of the palace, returning along St Andrew Street on the north side of the cathedral and passing ★★ **Vicar's Close**. This charming cobbled close was built in 1348 by

Bishop Ralph of Shrewsbury to house 'Members of the College of Vicars', clerics chosen for their singing voices. Over the gate is Vicar's Hall, where members dined, and at the far end of the street the chapel. Vicar's Hall is joined to the cathedral by the **Chain Bridge**.

Walking past the north side of the cathedral into Cathedral Green be sure to notice the exterior side of the clock, on which two medieval warriors mark time.

Glastonbury

From Wells, the A39 leads on to **Glastonbury** (population 6,800), the scene of an annual rock festival and the oldest Christian foundation in Britain. The ★★ **ruined abbey** (9.30am–6pm or dusk, if earlier; opens at 9am Jun–Aug and 10am Dec; admission charge) is built on the site of a much earlier church – according to legend dating from the 1st century, when Joseph of Arimethea is supposed to have brought either the Holy Grail or the Blood of the Cross here. St Patrick and St Bridget visited the abbey in the 5th century, and Edmund I (d. 946), Edgar (d. 975) and Edmund Ironside (d.1016) are all buried here. The buildings that you see date from between 1184 and 1303, when Glastonbury was the richest Benedictine abbey bar Westminster in England: they fell into ruins after the Dissolution. Remains of a warrior and his female companion, interred in front of the high altar, are identified as King Arthur and Queen Guinevere by local legend. Winter flowering hawthorns in the abbey's grounds are supposed to have sprung from the Holy Thorn borne here by Joseph. **Glastonbury Tor**, above the town, offers views as far as the Bristol Channel. It was here that the last abbot, Richard Whiting, and abbey treasurer, John Arthur Thorne, were executed in 1539 for opposing Henry VIII.

The ruined abbey

51

Just south of Glastonbury is **Street**, site of Millfield public school and the headquarters of the shoe company Clark's, founded in 1825 by wool dealer and rug-maker Cyrus Clark, who was soon running a profitable business making woollined slippers. Clark's Village (a factory-price outlet for well-known brands) includes a shoe museum.

A return to Bath along the picturesque A361 to **Shepton Mallet** (9 miles/5km from Glastonbury) passes the **Pilton Manor vineyards** (opportunities to buy local wine) and, 3 miles (5km) east of Shepton Mallet, Cranmore, departure point for the **East Somerset Steam Railway** (tel: 01749 880417 for timetable and booking). From Shepton Mallet, the A 37 passes Downside abbey and school to pick up the A367 to Bath via Radstock, where **Radstock, Midsomer Norton & District Museum** (Feb–Nov Tues–Fri, Sun and Bank Holiday Mon 2–5pm, Sat 11am–5pm) recalls 19th-century life in a north Somerset coalfield. The last coal was mined here in 1973.

East Somerset Steam Railway

Excursion 5

To Longleat and Stonehenge

Longleat – Warminster – Stonehenge – Stourhead *See map, p34–5*

Stonehenge

Longleat (22 miles/35 km from Bath), the home of the Marquess of Bath, is one of the southwest's top tourist attractions, as is Stonehenge, situated a further 14 miles (22 km) to the southeast. A full day is required for Longleat alone, especially if you want to see the Safari Park too; during school holidays it is advisable to arrive early.

Leave Bath along the A36 via Claverton Manor *(see Route 5)*. ★★**Longleat** (house: Easter–Sept daily 10am–5.30pm; rest of the year tours at set times between 11am–3pm; safari park: Apr–Oct 10am–4pm or 5pm on weekends, Bank Holidays and state school holidays; tel: 01985 844400; www.longleat.co.uk) is signposted from the roundabout at Beckington, about 20 miles (12 km) from Bath. There are a range of admission charges, depending on which attractions you want to visit. A 'passport ticket' grants access to all of them. Completely separate from the house and safari park, but occupying 400 acres of Longleat Forest (off the A36) is **Center Parcs**, (www.centerparcs.com), a family-oriented country-club-cum-theme-park where the theme is the great outdoors.

Henry Thynne, the 6th Marquess of Bath, opened Longleat to the public in 1949, a course of action partly necessitated by heavy death duties imposed after the death of the 5th Marquess in 1946. It was the first stately home to go public, but others soon followed suit. Since then Longleat has spawned into a huge entertainment complex attracting some 500,000 tourists a year. As well as the safari park (opened in 1966) there are safari boats to 'gorilla island' on the Half Mile Lake, a butterfly garden, a miniature railway, a Dr Who exhibition, a flight simulator, vintage cars, the 'world's largest maze' and a Postman Pat Village. The abiding pleasure of Longleat, however, is the vast parkland. Visitors can roam more or less as they please and fish in the lower reaches of the lake.

The wealthy Thynne family have modest roots. The founder of the dynasty, John Thynne (1515–80), began his working life as a clerk in the kitchen of the Tudor court. His prospects improved dramatically when, under the patronage of the Protector of Somerset, he was made a knight of the realm for his services in the battle against the Scots at Pinkie in 1547. With knighthood came prestige and wealth, and between 1559–80 he built Longleat. His grandson, Thomas Thynne, introduced royal blood to the

Longleat's miniature railway and the world's largest maze

line through his second marriage to Catherine Lyte Howard, descendant of the First Duke of Norfolk, whose ancestors included Edward I and Alfred the Great. In 1682, Thomas's grandson was made the 1st Viscount Weymouth, and in 1789 the 3rd Viscount Weymouth was made 1st Marquess of Bath by George III.

The first room you come to on entering the ★★ **house** and turning right from the reception is the ★★ **Great Hall**, a vast panelled room 35ft (10.6m) high, complete with a minstrels' gallery, which is the one room predominantly from the Elizabethan era; exhibits here include the blood-stained tunic worn by Charles I on his execution. Leading on from here is a series of ornate rooms, impeccably kept but with a comfortable, lived-in quality in spite of the opulence. Much of what you see was created in the Italian style by the designer J. D. Crace for the Fourth Marquess of Bath: the Lower East Corridor (fine 17th-century Flemish tapestries), the Italian-style Ante Library and Red Library, containing some of Longleat's 40,000 books, the Breakfast Room, Lower Dining Room (with Crace ceiling adapted from the Doge's Palace in Venice) and the sumptuous state rooms (dining room, saloon, drawing room and suite of state bedrooms). It was from the State Drawing Room that Titian's *Rest on the Flight to Egypt* was stolen in 1995. The painting was recovered in May 2003 and after a programme of restoration will go back on display.

Longleat House

Also open to the public (by appointment) are some of the corridors and halls covered in 3-D murals by the current Marquess, whose unconventional lifestyle frequently features in the tabloid press. Begun in the 1960s these murals now cover around a third of the house.

Among the attractions in the outbuildings is *The Life and Times of Lord Bath*, an exhibition dedicated to the Sixth Marquess with special emphasis on World War II. As well as Churchilliana there is a collection of watercolours by Adolf Hitler, whom the Sixth Marquess apparently admired.

The ★ **Safari Park** (admission charge) is a 15-minute drive from the house. It comprises a series of parkland enclosures in which, except in the areas where the animals are fairly harmless (giraffes, zebra, antelopes, etc), you are required to stay in your car with the windows closed (or take one of the special buses). The lions are the stars of the show.

From Longleat, the A36 leads south to Warminster (population: 15,000) and then, 17 miles (27km) further on, to Salisbury Plain, on which looms Britain's most evocative ancient monument, ★★★ **Stonehenge** (mid-Mar–end May 9.30am–6pm, Jun–end Aug 9am–7pm, Sept–mid-Oct 9.30am–6pm, mid Oct–mid-Mar 9.30am–4pm; admission charge), a UNESCO World Heritage site. Spanning the period 3,000–1,000 BC (the central ring of stones dates from around 2,000 BC), it comprises two types of stones – 123

One of the 'Lions of Longleat'

53

Stonehenge and Warminster

bluestones, hauled here from the Preseli mountains in Pembrokeshire, 200 miles (320km), and the larger sarsen stones which are found locally. Its purpose has baffled archaeologists and other experts for centuries and engendered many myths. Inigo Jones, one of the first to investigate its purpose, at the behest of James I, concluded it was a Roman temple to Uranus. Though the alignment of the major axis with the midsummer sunrise suggests a religious purpose, no firm evidence has been found, and theories range from the practical – a calendar – to the extraterrestrial.

There are long-term plans to divert the busy A303 running alongside the site and send it underground, a move designed to help restore an atmosphere of spirituality and a sense of dignity to the stones.

In the opposite direction along the B3092, about 3 miles (5km) north of Mere, is the village of Stourton and **★★ Stourhead** (house: Apr–Oct Fri–Tues 11am–5pm or dusk, closed Wed & Thur; garden: all year daily 9am–7pm or sunset; admission charges for house and garden), a Palladian mansion, now owned by the National Trust, built in 1721–24 by Colen Campbell. The estate is famous for its grounds, which represent one of the finest expressions of the early 18th-century landscape movement. A satisfying arrangement of formal gardens, dells, knolls, lake and parkland enfolds temples to Flora and Apollo, bridges, a cascade, a Gothic cottage, a grotto and the parish church, creating a delightful theatre for the changing seasons. Horace Walpole thought the gardens here 'one of the most picturesque scenes in the world'. On the west side of the garden a footpath leads for 2½ miles (4 km) to **Alfred's Tower** (Apr–Oct noon–5pm, Sat, Sun and Bank Holiday Mon 11.30am–5.30pm), an 18th-century brick folly, with views over the counties of Wiltshire, Somerset and Dorset, which all meet at this point.

Stourhead's grounds

Excursion 6

The Road to London

Corsham Court – Lacock Abbey – Sheldon Manor – Bowood House – Avebury Stone Circles *See map, p34–5*

Though designed as an excursion from Bath, the tour described here works just as well in reverse as part of a leisurely day's drive from London (take the M4 as far as Chieveley (junction 13), then the A4 through Newbury, Hungerford and Marlborough.

The A4 was the main route to London for centuries before the M4 was built. It links a series of old English towns important to the medieval cloth trade – as was Bath – and it was along here that the London stage coach brought many of Bath's 18th-century visitors. In 1667 it took three days for a coach to make the journey from London to Bath, but by 1711 the time had been cut to between 30 and 38 hours, providing the journey wasn't interrupted by highwaymen and heavy luggage was taken separately. Reflecting its historical importance, the road has a number of grand 18th-century estates within easy striking distance, and these form the core of this tour.

Leaving Bath via Bathampton (a pretty village also accessible by boat from Bath Boating Station, *see page 71*) the road climbs to Box.

Off to the right, some 15km (9 miles) from Bath, is **★★ Corsham Court** (last week Mar–end Sept 2–5pm, closed Mon; rest of the year (except Dec) weekends only 2–5.30pm; admission charge), the delightful informality of which– characterful retainers, peacocks mooching in the hallway, the master's dogs seeking titbits – was captured in a cameo documentary by the BBC shortly before the death of the Sixth Lord Methuen in 1995.

Corsham Court

The current building dates from 1582, when it was built on or near the site of an ancient manor house that had served as a country retreat for Saxon kings. It came into the hands of the Methuen family in 1745, after which its north (rear) side gained a Palladian facade (later replaced). In around 1760 it was enlarged by Capability Brown, who duplicated the wings on the south front and converted the east wing into a suite of state rooms (open to the public today). Further changes were made in 1800 when John Nash replaced the Palladian-style north front with a building in the style of Strawberry Hill Gothic, but this was substantially changed again in the 1840s by the architect Thomas Bellamy, in an attempt to rid the house of damp.

The chief treasures of Corsham are its paintings, many of them acquired by Sir Paul Methuen (1672–1757), the godfather of the Methuen who bought Corsham. All the rooms contain fine works of art, but the **Picture Gallery**, hung with red silk damask, was specially designed by Capability Brown to house Sir Paul's collection. Highlights here include Van Dyck's *Betrayal of Christ* and *A Man in a Ruff*, works by Bernardo Strozzi and Borgognone, and Sofonisba Anguisciola's attractive *Three Gaddi Children*. Complementing the paintings is furniture by Chippendale and the Adam brothers, whose handiwork also graces the other rooms. More paintings are found in the **Cabinet Room**, including an exquisite Annunciation from the studio of Fra Filippo Lippi and the *Flying Cherub*, a cartoon by Cesari for a mosaic in the cupola of St Peter's in Rome; and the **State Bedroom**, containing a portrait of Pope Gregory XV by Reni. The **Octagon Room** includes *The Sleeping Cupid* (1496), attributed (dubiously) to Michelangelo in the catalogue, and an allegorical portrait by an unknown artist of a troubled Elizabeth I flanked by death and having her crown removed by two cherubs – supposedly referring to her feelings of remorse following the execution of her former favourite, Robert Devereux, Earl of Essex.

56

Outside, gravel walks lead to a **Bath House**, designed by Capability Brown, with its 15th-century **Bradford Porch**, taken from a house called The Priory in Bradford-on-Avon *(see page 38)*, where the Methuen family's wool business was based. Also in the village of Corsham (in *House in Corsham* Park Lane) is the **Underground Quarry** (Apr and Oct Sun only; May–Sept daily except Fri; closed in winter) where guided tours of the shaft stone mine trace the history of mining the characteristic Bath stone.

House in Corsham

A few miles further along the A4 (14miles/22km from Bath), the A350 leads off to Lacock Abbey in the delightfully unspoilt village of **Lacock**. Lacock's immediate appeal lies not only in its quaint architecture, but in its lack, thanks to the National Trust which owns the village, of telegraph wires, poles and road markings. For this reason it has been a location in a number of films and television costume dramas, and served as Meryton in the BBC's acclaimed 1995 production of *Pride and Prejudice*.

Lacock Abbey entrance and cloisters

★★**Lacock Abbey** (National Trust; Apr–Oct 1–5.30pm, closed Tues), an intriguing mix of medieval, Renaissance and Gothic architecture, was founded in 1232 by Ela Countess of Salisbury as a nunnery for Augustinian canonesses. Following the Dissolution of the Monasteries in 1539 Henry VIII pensioned off the nuns and sold the property to William Sharrington, who set about converting it into a home. Sharrington's conversion retained many of the original features of the 13th-century abbey, including the buildings flanking the clois-

ter court. He partitioned the nuns' refectory and dormitories to create the Brown Gallery and Stone Gallery and added the octagonal tower and swizzlestick chimney stacks. Much of the fine masonry of this period is attributed to John Chapman, mason to Henry VIII.

Cloister window

Later, in the mid-18th century, John Ivory Talbot commissioned Sanderson Miller, the architect who inspired the fashion for follies, to make alterations in the Gothic style – pointed-arch windows, medieval style masonry – in harmony with the building's ecclesiastical origins. The **Hall** was remodelled, with ogee-arched niches containing terracotta statuettes and a ceiling covered in the coats of arms of Talbot's friends and neighbours. In the 19th century Talbot's great grandson, William Henry Fox Talbot, altered the south side, introducing the oriel windows.

Fox Talbot had a keen interest in the sciences. As well as being a respected botanist, he made important contributions to the development of photography. In 1840 he discovered the calotype process, in which an image is produced on paper treated with silver iodide and developed by sodium thiosulphite. His negative of an oriel window in Lacock's South Gallery is the oldest in existence. The abbey's barn houses the **Fox Talbot Museum of Photography** (Mar–Oct 11am–5.30pm, closed Tues, Nov–Dec weekends only 11am–4pm, closed for a period over Christmas).

57

The **Cloister** is flanked by 14th- and 15th-century rooms belonging to the original nunnery, including the Chaplain's Room (on the south walk) and the Sacristy, Chapter House and Warming Room (east walk). The stone coffins in the latter were found in the grounds.

The village of **Lacock** is enchanting. Standing out among its 13th-century stone and half-timbered cottages is the imposing red-brick Red Lion inn (good food, plus accommodation), next door to which is a tiny museum dedicated to packaging. Here, you can enjoy the nostalgia conjured up by the labels of yesteryear, from Zebo black grate polish to favourite childhood confectionery.

Sheldon Manor inside and out

On the north side of the A4, signposted off the A420 2½ miles (4km) from Chippenham, are the romantic gardens of **Sheldon Manor** (gardens only: Easter–Oct Sun, Thurs and Bank Holidays 2–6pm), the only surviving building of a medieval village. A little further afield (3 miles/5km) in this direction, off the B4039, is **Castle Combe**, the archetypal Cotswold village, much visited by tourists but retaining most of its charm.

Close to the village is the **Castle Combe Skid Pan and Kart Track** (tel: 01249 783010) where an open grand prix is held on the first Saturday of every month.

The last of the grand houses on this tour is ★★ **Bowood**

Bowood House and gardens

House (house: Apr–Oct daily 11am–5.30pm, grounds 11am–6pm; admission charge), 2½ miles (4km) off the A4, a few miles east of Chippenham. The Palladian home of the Earl and Countess of Shelburne, it offers a fine interior, including the laboratory where Dr Joseph Priestley discovered oxygen; extensive grounds and a well designed adventure playground for children. What you see today is only a part of the original house. The 'Big House', formerly adjoining the eastern end, was demolished in 1955.

Entrance is through the **orangery**, designed by Robert Adam in 1769. Adam was employed by the 1st Marquess of Lansdowne to complete an existing, unfinished house which his father had bought in 1754. Once filled with tubs of orange and lemon trees, this long, light gallery was used for special occasions. During a royal visit by King Edward VII and Queen Alexandria in 1907 it was decked out with palms and a Persian tent. A number of the cabinets are filled with mementoes relating to the 5th Lord of Lansdowne's term as Viceroy of India (1888–94), including letters from Queen Victoria.

Off the orangery (turn right as you enter the house) is the **laboratory** in which oxygen was discovered (1774) by Dr Joseph Priestley, the librarian and tutor to the two sons of the 1st Lord Lansdowne. Lansdowne, a flamboyant character who served as prime minister for a while (he was described by Disraeli as 'the ablest and most accomplished statesman of the 18th century') patronised the arts and sciences. Bowood's laboratory was later used by John Ingenhouse who discovered photosynthesis and helped develop inoculation against smallpox.

The **library** was designed by Robert Adam in 1769, but was substantially altered by the architect C. R. Cockerell in 1821–24, including the coffered ceiling. In the middle of the orangery two bronze doors lead to the private

chapel, also remodelled by Cockerell, which is still used for special services today. Highlights in the exhibition rooms upstairs include the Albanian costume worn by Lord Byron and the **Lansdowne Napoleonic Collection** containing Napoleon's bronze death mask.

The **grounds** of Bowood are suitably grand, and especially delightful in spring when the rhododendrons and azaleas bloom (the rhododendron park is open during the flowering season between mid-April to early June). The long lake below the terraces was created by Capability Brown in the 1760s. Its north end features a Doric temple, cascade and 'hermit's cave', all added at a later date. A fine mausoleum, designed by Adam, stands in the rhododendron park.

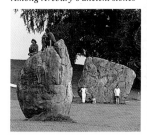

Striking a pose in Bowood's grounds

From Calne (19 miles/30km from Bath) the A4 crosses the chalk Downs (notice **Lansdowne Column** and a 'white horse', one of several hereabouts which was carved in 1780 on the hill to the right), which together with Salisbury Plain forms one of the richest prehistoric landscapes in Europe. It is dotted with the dolmens and standing stones of Iron Age farmers. ★★ **Avebury Stone Circle** (free admission to view stones), 1 mile (2km) north of the A4 is the largest circle in Britain. Hauled here from Marlborough Downs, 3 miles (5km) away, some 4,000 years ago, the sarsen stones (extremely hard-wearing sandstone found scattering the downs and Salisbury Plain) form one large circle surrounded by a ditch (originally twice as deep as it is today) and two sets of smaller concentric circles (spanned by Avebury village which has grown up among the stones). The site was used for ceremonial purposes, a role revived by Druids and New Agers at the winter and summer solstices and spring and autumn equinoxes. A concrete post in the centre of an inner circle marks the spot of the Obelisk, a tall thin stone around which human bones have been found. Also of interest in the village is the 17th-century Great Barn holding a museum of rural life and Avebury Manor (National Trust), a late 16th-century building with Queen Anne alterations.

59

Among Avebury's ancient stones

Back on the A4, a few miles further on, the road passes the mysterious **Silbury Hill** (on the left), the largest manmade mound in Europe (purpose unknown), and, signposted across fields to the right, **West Kennet Long Barrow Tomb**, 5,000 years old and one of the largest chambered tombs in Britain. Access is allowed into part of the tomb, where votive offerings to Pan are sometimes found – an ear of wheat, a daisy, a lighted candle.

Silbury Hill

This tour ends at the attractive market town of **Marlborough**, whose colonnaded high street offers a lively central market and a clutch of good tea-shops popular with pupils at the town's famous public school.

Architecture

The Palladian style

The style of architecture exemplified by Bath is known as Palladian, after the late-Renaissance Venetian architect Andrea Palladio (1508–80), whose buildings and writings inspired the style. Palladio's own inspiration (Venice's Il Redentore and San Giorgio Maggiore churches and the Teatro Olimpico) was the architecture of ancient Greece and Rome, the governing principles of which were symmetry and proportion, as laid down by Vetruvius, the author of the only work on architecture to survive from Roman times. There were five styles of classical architecture (the Five Orders): Doric, Ionic, Corinthian, Tuscan and Composite (a mixture of Corinthian and Ionic), each represented by its pillars, which dictated the proportions of the style as a whole. These proportions not only applied to the facade of a building, but also to its interior, where the position of skirting, dado and cornice all had to mirror the proportions of the classical column.

Palladianism was first introduced to Britain by Inigo Jones as early as 1620. It was revived a century later, around 1715, when Lord Burlington brought the Venetian architect Giacomo Leoni to England to work on a book of Palladio's designs. This book, along with a volume called *Vitruvius Britannicus* by the architect Colin Campbell, became a pattern book not only for architects but also for master builders.

61

The John Woods

The architect credited with introducing the Palladian style to Bath is John Wood the Elder (1704–54), who had worked with Palladian architects in London. Though individual Palladian buildings had already been erected in the city (for example, General Wolfe's House, at No 5 Trim Street), he conceived of whole streets and terraces in the Palladian style, an ambition Bath's urgent need for accommodation made viable. What's more, Bath's growing fashionableness among England's upper classes made a grandiose style of architecture appropriate.

Queen Square and the Royal Mineral Water Hospital

Partly inspired by Bath's Roman heritage (even though most of Aquae Sulis was unexcavated at the time), Wood envisaged a 'Royal Forum', a 'Grand Circus' and an 'Imperial Gymnasium'. In the end, diverted by other projects such as Prior Park *(see page 44)*, he achieved only a small part of this dream: Queen Square (1729–39), the North and South parades (1740–43), the Royal Mineral Water Hospital (1742), and the Circus (1754–67), which his son, John Wood the Younger, completed.

John Wood the Younger embraced his father's vision totally. He transformed the Upper Town, then bordering

Royal Crescent

on countryside, into the preferred residential area for people of taste and wealth. The whole focus of Bath society shifted as a result. After completing his father's circus in 1767 he went on to create the Royal Crescent (1767–74) and the New Assembly Rooms (1769–1771). The steep gradients of the Upper Town created technical problems, but these were solved by excavating the hillsides and building a level platform beneath each property. In some cases problems could not be overcome. Camden Crescent (John Eveleigh, 1788) was never completed because of land slippage, hence its off-centre pediment.

From Palladian to neoclassical and Gothic

The Palladian style is so pervasive in Bath for two reasons: firstly, the need for rapid expansion during the 18th century and secondly the fact that the dramatic contours of the city lent visual variety to the terraces and crescents and saved the style from becoming boring. Added to this was the ready availability of Bath stone following the opening of Ralph Allen's quarries on Combe Down. The soft limestone blocks could be easily shaped by the mason's chisel and together created a perfectly smooth facade which looked like a single piece of stone (though this was only deemed necessary for the front facade – the backs of Bath's buildings were often undressed rubble).

However, Palladianism wasn't totally static. Buildings from the first half of the century are different in many ways from those at the end. Decorative baroque details around doors and windows, popular until about 1730 (Wood's Queen Square), gave way to much plainer frames, and by the end of the 1760s there was virtually no detail at all. The Circus, with its decorative frieze and parapet, are in contrast to the plain Royal Crescent which derives its impact from its commanding position and great sweep of 114 Ionic columns. In addition, despite the great pains taken by the architects and builders to create seamless facades, householders still liked to put their own individual stamp on a building, perhaps with a more elaborate doorway to reflect their greater prestige.

But by the 1770s the tide was turning and Palladianism, with its clean straight lines, was developing into neoclassicism, a less rigorous interpretation of the classical style with finer decorative details and more graceful lines, exemplified by the architect and furniture-designer Robert Adam. This change was partly prompted by architects going abroad on the Grand Tour and seeing the ruins of the Greek and Roman civilisations for themselves. Robert Adam had studied in Rome, but instead of directly copying what he had seen there, he used the motifs and ideas as a springboard for his imagination.

Heavily influenced by Adam was Thomas Baldwin

Corinthian columns (above) and Ionic columns (below)

(most of the development on the east side of Pulteney Bridge, the Guildhall, Bath Street and the Cross Bath. Compare John Wood the Younger's austere Hot Bath (1778) with Baldwin's nearby Cross Bath (1780s), with its sinuous curves and finely carved friezes. Other architects active in Bath at the time were John Palmer (Lansdown Crescent 1789–93, the Grand Pump Room) and John Eveleigh (Camden Crescent 1788, Somerset Place 1790).

Georgian window and the Guildhall

Meanwhile, from the mid-18th century Gothic elements crept in, adding a romantic twist. Ogee windows can sometimes be found in an otherwise classical facade. Bath's most notable example of Gothic is the Countess of Huntingdon's Chapel (1765), with its castellated parapet and ogee-arched windows.

The Gothic style was especially appropriate to garden architecture, which became increasingly popular as gardens grew larger and, in the country at least, incorporated parkland, lakes and streams. The ubiquitous temples, obelisks and 'pantheons' were often relieved by a Gothic feature or two, as at Stourhead *(see page 54)*. And Gothic ruins and follies were fashionable until well into the 19th century. In Bath, Ralph Allen hired Sanderson Miller to build the Gothic Sham Castle (1762) on Claverton Down, and Bath eccentric William Beckford had Lansdown Tower (1827) built, a 154-ft (53-m) high tower-cum-minaret, on the top of Lansdown Hill.

63

The interiors

As a rule, Bath interiors are rather plain, even though Georgian houses in other cities are often quite lavish inside. Most housing was intended for short-stay guests, in town for the season, and landlords were loath to waste money on unnecessary ornament. The obvious exceptions are the great public buildings such as the Assembly Rooms and the Guildhall and fine houses specifically built for their occupants. In the case of the Assembly Rooms, the splendid interior is in marked contrast to the plain exterior: in the ballroom, decorated friezes, a plinth mounted by 12-ft (3.6-m) high Corinthian columns, and Vitruvian scrollwork; in the tea room Ionic and Corinthian columns, gilded iron railings, and coves decorated with carvings of foliage. Incidentally, these rooms are painted in colours (a warm yellow and dark peppermint) appropriate to the period.

During the latter half of the century internal walls were plastered rather than panelled, making the delicate decorative details favoured by Adam easier to achieve. The Banqueting Hall of Baldwin's Guildhall, heavily influenced by Adam, is filled with exquisitely carved details. Following the birth of publications such as the monthly *Builder's Magazine* Adam's designs were widely imitated.

Guildhall interior

Victorian adjustments

The Georgian period came to an end in 1830. The Victorians, whose forte was industrial design, had less clearly defined ideas about architecture. Grand buildings were built in any one of several revivalist styles, with neoclassical jostling with Greek revival and Gothic. Ordinary housing for the growing middle and lower-middle classes was supplied by bay-windowed villas, which spread in ribbons south and west of the city, entwining many old villages in the process.

The Victorians are blamed for spoiling many of the Georgian facades by 'building out' (Adam's Pulteney Bridge, for example, acquired ugly extensions, still seen on the unrestored rear side). And whereas the Georgians had been careful to conceal drainpipes, either taking them down the back of buildings or hiding them in the front walls, the Victorians had fewer aesthetic scruples. Sometimes they painted the facades, by then black from pollution, and often tampered with their proportions, extending the length of windows to let in more light and replacing the small panes of Georgian glass with sheet glass.

But attempts were made to adapt some Georgian buildings sensitively. J. M. Brydon extended the Guildhall and added the Victoria Art Gallery. He also added the domed concert hall to the Pump Room and was responsible for incorporating the newly excavated Great Bath into the Pump Room and King's Bath ensemble. Similarly, great efforts were made to integrate the Kennet and Avon Canal (1810) and the Great Western Railway (1840). Though both of these cut right through the city they don't detract from its beauty.

Post World War II

In World War II Bath was hit by the Baedeker raids, a bombing campaign aimed at cities of outstanding cultural significance. A heavy programme of restoration ensued, in many cases taking decades to complete. Where the damage was beyond repair, and sometimes simply in the name of making the city more suited to 20th-century living, the old was swept away and replaced by modern shops and offices. Though in Bath stone (or artificial Bath stone), as dictated by the Bath Act of 1925, the new buildings were almost universally disliked, provoking a barrage of opposition to future redevelopments. Nowadays, Bath's planners chart a difficult course between conservation and regeneration, resulting in some peculiar hybrids such as the Podium, in Northgate Street. What's more, tastes change. What was deemed hideous and fit only for demolition a decade or two ago may suddenly be championed by new aesthetic values – which is exactly what happened to the Empire Hotel, an Edwardian pile overlooking Parade Gardens.

64

Victoria Art Gallery and the dome of the Pump Room's concert hall

The Arts

Bath has had a vigorous cultural life ever since Beau Nash introduced a small orchestra comprising six London-trained musicians in the early 1700s. Today, several city arts festivals have gained an international reputation, but even on an everyday level the city lives and breathes music and performance art. Abbey Churchyard is a stage for fire-eaters, jugglers and clowns, while street musicians – from African drummers to string quartets – are encountered at every turn. On summer weekends music fills the city's parks.

Music: venues and festivals

Events are regularly held in the Assembly Rooms, the Pump Room, the Guildhall, the Abbey and at the American Museum at Claverton (for details, consult *This Month in Bath,* free from the Tourist Information Centre, or the *Bath Chronicle*, which also has a useful website, www. thisisbath.com).

Bath International Music Festival (mid-May to early June) is a two-week programme of concerts held in venues throughout Bath. One of Britain's most important music festivals, it attracts classical and jazz performers from across the world. A little later, in mid-July and early August, the International Guitar Festival offers everything from flamenco and classical to blues and finger-style acoustic.

Jazz performer and Bath Festival Concert

65

For programme details of all these festivals and others contact the website www. bathfestivals.org.uk or the box office, tel: 01225 463362.

Literary events

Bath Literature Festival (February or early March) includes readings, plays, talks and performances, with around 50 percent of the programme aimed at children. For details, contact the website www.bathlitfest.org.uk.

There is also a Jane Austen festival in September; at other times Austen fans can join a walking tour of places associated with the author. The tours (summer daily 1.30pm, winter weekends only; charge made) last 1½ hours and depart from Abbey Churchyard.

Theatre, Cabaret and Comedy

The Theatre Royal has a varied programme, consistently featuring well-known actors and actresses, while the nearby Ustinov Studio in Monmouth Street stages smaller productions and workshops for children and adults (box office for both theatres, tel: 01225 448844; www.theatreroyal.org.uk). Backstage tours of the first Wednesday and Saturday of the month.

Cabaret and comedy are celebrated at the Fringe Festival, held around the same time as the music festival.

Fringe Festival act

Food and Drink

Bath has two claims to fame on the culinary front: the Bath bun, which is much in evidence in its tea-rooms, and the Bath Oliver biscuit, a white biscuit invented by Dr William Oliver in the 18th century to suit the delicate digestion of invalids and now, thanks to the entrepreneurial instincts of the doctor's coachman, to whom Oliver bequeathed the secret recipe, the perfect companion to Stilton cheese. But there are several more recherché specialities to be discovered, including the Bath sausage (fresh pork, Wiltshire bacon, spinach and Dijon mustard), available from the **Sausage Shop** (7 Green Street) and traditional local cheeses such as Tornegus (a soft Caerphilly-type cheese), sold by **Paxton & Whitfields** (1 John Street, corner of Quiet Street; with Café Fromage serving cheese-based dishes and baguettes upstairs). Lastly, there is **Sally Lunn's** bun (surprisingly light and digestible in spite of its vast dimensions) invented by Bath baker Sally Lunn in around 1680. Infinitely versatile, the Lunn bun comes in many different guises – from a platform for Welsh rarebit or chicken curry to a fluffy underpinning for strawberry jam and clotted cream.

South of Bath, there is no escaping West Country specialities such as cider and Cheddar cheese, which have become an integral part of the region's tourist industry. These and other specialites are represented at Bath's Farmer's Market, held in the restored Green Park Station on the first and third Saturday in the month. You can also look out for local wines, such as those from Pilton Manor vineyards *(see page 51)* and the local, award-winning Bellringer beer.

In keeping with the city's long tradition of providing pleasures the city has many restaurants. They range from the esteemed Hole in the Wall offering the best in modern British cooking to spicy Mai-Thai. Wherever you dine, be sure to book, especially in summer and on weekends.

Restaurants

£££ expensive (over £60 for two); **££** moderate (£40–60 for two); **£** inexpensive (under £40 for two). Price brackets are for two courses, plus a bottle of house wine.

The Hole in the Wall

Circus Restaurant, 34 Brock Street, tel: 01225 318918. Upmarket British/French cuisine in fine setting. **££**
Demuth's, 2 North Parade, tel: 01225 446059. Long-established, very good vegetarian restaurant. Licensed. **£**
Eastern Eye, 8a Quiet Street, tel: 01225 422323. Fine Indian cuisine in a Georgian interior. **££**
Green Park Brasserie, Green Park Road, tel: 01225 338565. Well cooked British/French dishes. Lively atmosphere with occasional jazz. **££**

The Olive Tree

The Hole in the Wall, 16 George Street, tel: 01225 425242. A long-established restaurant which has been revived to great acclaim. Imaginative modern British cuisine. **£££**

Mai Thai, 6 Pierrepont Street, tel: 01225 445557. Excellent Thai in Georgian setting. **££**

The Moody Goose, 7a Kingsmead Square, tel: 01225 466688. Michelin-starred restaurant serving modern British and French food. **£££**

The Moon and Sixpence, 6a Broad Street, tel: 01225 460962. Modern British food, plus some foreign imports. Old favourites are given an imaginative twist. Courtyard for summer dining. **££**

The Olive Tree, Queensberry Hotel, Russel Street, tel: 01225 447928. 'Foodie' favourite, serving modern British cooking, with French, Italian and Moroccan influences. Situated below the Queensberry Hotel. **£££**

Pizza Express, 1-4 Barton Street, tel: 01225 420119. Branch of the popular chain next door to the Theatre Royal. **£**

The Pump Room, Stall Street, tel: 01225 444477. Morning coffee, lunches, set teas and evening meals in July and August. Come for the ambience rather than the food, which is nothing special. **£–££**

Rajpoot, 4 Argyle Street, tel: 01225 466833. First-rate cooking from Rajasthan. **££**

The Royal Crescent Hotel, Royal Crescent, tel: 01225 823333. Within the walled gardens of the hotel. Superb food and elegant surroundings. **£££**

Sally Lunn's, 4 North Parade Passage, tel: 01225 461634. An excellent option for a lunchtime snack, but poor value during the evening, when the tea-room converts to a candlelit restaurant. **£** at lunchtime, **££** in the evening.

Woods, 9–13 Alfred Street, tel: 01225 314812. British and French cuisine in elegant surroundings in the Upper Town. **££–£££**

Inside the Moon and Sixpence

Shopping

Compact, diverse and with a number of luxury shops not normally found outside London, Bath has the best shopping centre in southwest England. It has done for centuries. Several of Jane Austen's characters are depicted shopping in its lanes. In *Northanger Abbey* Isabella Thorpe, 'saw the prettiest hat you can imagine, in a shop window in Milsom Street', and in *Persuasion* Sir Walter stands in a shop in Bond Street and counts 87 women go by with 'not one tolerable face among them'.

South of the Pump Room

Generally, the higher you climb in Bath, the more exclusive the shops. The area below the Pump Room is dominated by mainstream chain stores (Marks & Spencer, British Home Stores, Boots). There are, however, notable exceptions, including Rose Marie, on **Abbey Green**, offering ladies who lunch elegant outfits for special occasions, and in **Manvers Street**, down by the railway station, George Bayntum, one of the world's leading antiquarian bookshops and binderies, established in 1829.

Northumberland Passage
George Bayntum, antiquarian books

North of the Pump Room

In **Abbey Churchyard** you will find several shops aimed primarily at tourists, including the National Trust Shop and a branch of the English Teddy Bear Company. More original on **Orange Grove**, east of the Abbey, is the Glass House studio selling contemporary glassware.

North of Westgate, Union Street leads on to Old Bond Street and then Milsom Street *(see below)* in one long shopping thoroughfare, with fruitful side streets such as **Northumberland Passage**, **Union Passage** and **Shires Yard** (designer labels, expensive lingerie, and fine shoes). At the top of Union Street (Disney Store, Next, County Casuals) **Upper Borough Walls** harbours Susan Gillis-Browne, a classsy dress shop, and the chain Monsoon. Here Burton Street turns into **New Bond Street** where, alongside Habitat, Laura Ashley, Jigsaw, Karen Millen and Warehouse cater to different dress senses.

Old Bond Street and **Milsom Street** offer a roll-call of well-known names, including Gap, Hobbs, Gieves & Hawkes, Bally, Waterstone's, Hobb's, Austin Reed, Jaeger, Culpeper, Jackpot, The Field (menswear) and the Savoy Taylors Guild. Also here is the much-loved 19th-century department store Jolly's.

Higher still are high-class purveryors of furnishings, antiques and fine art, many specialising in 18th-century items. For a run-down (including locator map) of the many antique shops in the Upper Town obtain the leaflet 'Bath & Bradford on Avon antique Dealers Association' from

Get ahead hats in Rose Marie

Walcot Street fleamarket

the Tourist Information Centre. Even if you are not interested in antiques it is worth walking up to the Great Western Antique Centre in **Bartlett Street**. Jessie's Button Box sells buttons and clasps from the 18th century to the present day.

High Street, Broad Street and Walcot Street

This area is worth exploring for offbeat shops. **Broad Street** offers Rossiters department store, while its upper reaches have several soft furnishings and interior design shops In **Green Street**, leading off Broad Street, is the Sausage Shop.

Leading up to the London Road from the High Street, **Walcot Street** is a rich hunting-ground for crafts, antiques, junk and wrought-ironwork, as well as being the location for the well-known toy-shop Tridias (No 124). Haliden Oriental Rugs has a large selection of antique items, and further up, Walcot Reclamation specialises in architectural antiques and unusual garden furniture. On Saturdays, a fleamarket is held in the warehouse next to Walcot car park on Walcot Street. At 105–107 Walcot Street is Bath Aqua, Theatre of Glass, where factory seconds can be bought cheaply.

Bridge Street and Pulteney Bridge

Just before the bridge Droopy & Browns offers romantic evening wear. Around the corner on **Grand Parade** (next to the entrance to Guildhall Market, a traditional indoor market, worth dipping into) is Long Tall Sally, selling well-made clothes for tall women. The shops on the **bridge** itself are generally too tiny to offer anything very interesting, but there is the Bath Stamp and Coin Shop, a good quality florist, the Antique Map Shop and, on the far side of the bridge, the Bath Rugby Shop, selling shirts, scarves and other memorabilia.

Active Pursuits

Ballooning

One of the most memorable views of Bath is from a balloon. Bath Balloon Flights, 8 Lambridge Road, BA1 6BT, tel: 01225 466888; www.bathballoons.co.uk, operates year round. Balloons are launched from Royal Victoria Park; flights last about 1 hour.

Ballooning over Bath

Boating

On the Avon, the Boating Station, Forester Road (signposted from Sydney Gardens) hires out traditional wooden rowing boats, punts and canoes by the hour or day between April and September (March and October weekends only). Tel: 01225 428844. Organised river trips run to Bathampton Weir and back (1 hour) from below Pulteney Bridge.

The Kennet and Avon Canal Trust operates narrow-boat cruises from Bath Top Lock (tel: 01225 462313). For self-drive cruises through the lovely Limpley Stoke Valley, the Bath & Dundas Canal Co (Brass Knocker Bottom, Monkton Combe, tel: 01225 722292), 5 miles (8km) southeast of Bath (off the A36), has small electrically-powered boats for between four and 10 passengers.

Messing about in boats

Caving

Cheddar Caves and Gorge runs caving, climbing and abseiling expeditions for anyone aged 12–60. Full equipment is provided; trainers required for abseiling. Tel: 01934 742343.

Fishing

Chew and Blagdon lakes, off the A368 west of Bath, offer good fly fishing for rainbow and brown trout Mar–Oct. Boats may be hired for the day (book in advance). Though the lakes are popular with very experienced anglers, novices are welcome, with beginners days, casting lessons and tuition weeks available. Contact: Woodford Lodge, Chew Stoke, Bristol BS18 8XH, tel: 01275 332339

Golf

Bath Golf Club, Sham Castle. 18-hole course open to non-members (with handicap certificate) except at weekends; equipment may be hired. Tel: 01225 463834.

Bowood House (*see page 58*) also offers an 18-hole golf course, set in Capability Brown's Bowood Great Park. Open to non-members. Tel: 01249 822228.

Pony trekking

Wellow Trekking Centre, Little Horse Croft Farm, Wellow. A range of rides available. Open year round, except Christmas Day. Tel: 01225 834376.

Getting There

By car
Bath lies within easy reach of both the M4 and M5 motorways, making it easily accessible from London, Wales and the Midlands. However, the lovely countryside around the city can make slower 'A' roads more attractive options, in particular the A4 across the Wiltshire Downs (*see page 55*) and the A46 which winds through the Cotswolds from Stroud and Cheltenham.

By coach
National Express runs a direct coach service between London Victoria bus station and Bath every 1–2 hours, as well as services from many other towns and cities. The journey from London takes around 3¼hrs (tel: 08705 808080; website: *www.gobycoach.com).*

Bath's bus station is opposite the train station, on the south side of town, a short walk from the centre.

By train
Great Western (*www.greatwestern.co.uk*) operates a fast service between London Paddington and Bath Spa (from 1hr 20 minutes) and Bristol Temple Meads (1hr 40 minutes). Wales and Borders (www.walesandborders.co.uk) operates trains to Bath from London Waterloo (around 2 hours). For all rail enquiries contact National Rail Enquiries, tel: 0845 7484950.

Bath Spa Station

Bath Spa Station is to the south of the city centre (an eight-minute walk from the Abbey). It is served by a taxi rank and has a branch of Hertz on the premises.

By air
The nearest airport is Bristol (north of the city, near the junction of the M4 and M5 motorways. Airport information: 0870 1212747.

73

Getting Around

Bath is a compact city best suited to walking. A variety of maps are available from the Tourist Information Centre in Abbey Churchyard. The open-top bus tours which offer an all-day hop on and off service can be a useful way of getting around (*see Facts for Visitor, page 75*).

Car Rental
It is worth hiring a car if you want to explore the countryside and villages around Bath. Car rental firms include:
   National Car Rental, tel: 01225 481898
   Hertz, tel: 01225 337759/442911

Buses

Though unlikely to be necessary in the city centre, buses can be useful for making short trips to sites such as Beckford's Tower, Prior Park, the American Museum at Claverton and nearby villages, such as Bradford-on-Avon. For information, contact the bus station, tel: 01225 464446 (www.firstbadgerline.co.uk). Be aware that a return ticket is the same price as a single and also that you can buy a day pass offering considerable savings.

Trains

The easiest option

Trains to Bristol Temple Meads (not Bristol Parkway, which is some way from the city centre) leave from Bath Spa Station throughout the day and take between 15 and 25 minutes depending on the type of train. National rail enquiries: 0845 748950. Look out for special passes such as the First Bus & Rail Card, which offers all-day travel on First Great Western trains and buses.

Taxis

Taxi ranks are found at Bath Spa station, the Orange Grove, Milsom Street and New Orchard Street. It is sensible to book taxis in advance on Friday and Saturday evenings.

Abbey Radio Taxis: 01225 465843
Ace Taxis: 01225 427411
D C Travel: 01225 425678
Orange Grove Taxis: 01225 447777
Rainbow Taxis: 01225 460606

Bike hire with a difference

Bike hire

Bikes can be hired from Avon Valley Cyclery, behind Bath Spa Station, tel: 01225 461880/442442. The towpath of the Kennet and Avon canal offers easy, safe cycling. In Bradford-on-Avon, bikes can be hired from Lock Inn Cottage, 48 Frome Road, tel: 01225 868068.

Car parks

Parking is difficult in Bath. Park & Ride schemes – Newbridge Road (Mon–Sat), Bath University (Sat only), Lansdown playing fields (weekdays only), Odd Down (Mon–Sat) – try to dissuade visitors from bringing vehicles into the city centre. Parking is free (there is a small charge for the ride) and buses leave at regular intervals.

On-street parking is very restricted, and many streets are now residents-only zones. Illegally parked cars will be clamped or removed. Car parks are found at the following locations: Avon Street, Charlotte Street (below Royal Victoria Park), Walcot Street, the Podium (Walcot Street with a three-hour limit), Ham Gardens (near the bus station), Manvers Street (near South Parade) and Sports Centre and Bath Cricket Club (both near the North Parade).

Facts for the Visitor

Tourist Information

The Tourist Information Centre is located in Abbey Churchyard. The staff can help with a wide range of enquiries on both Bath and the surrounding area, and offer a room booking service. Tel: 01225 477101.

Outside Bath
Bradford on Avon, tel: 01225 865797
Bristol, tel: 0906 586 2313 (higher rate)
Cheddar, tel: 01934 744071
Glastonbury, tel: 01458 832954
Warminster, tel: 01985 218548
Wells, tel: 01749 672552

Take the tour bus route or devise your own

75

Left luggage

Neither the train station nor the bus station offers left luggage facilities. However, Backpackers, a friendly hostel at 13 Pierrepont Street (tel: 01225 446787), a couple of minutes' walk from both stations, will store baggage for £2 an item. You do not need to be staying in the hostel to use the service.

Travel services

American Express, 5 Bridge Street, tel: 01225 444800; foreign exchange 01225 444767.

Sightseeing tours

Open-top bus tours (either Citytour or The Bath Bus Company) offer a hop-on-and-off ticket valid all day, so can be a useful way of getting from one sight to another. In addition, Tuk-Tuk Tours offers one-hour tours of the city by tuk-tuk, a mode of transport associated with Bangkok (tel: 01225 425866; www.tuktuktours.co.uk).

Guided walks are led by the Mayor's Honorary Guides.

They leave from outside the Pump Room in Abbey Churchyard Sun–Fri 10.30am and 2pm (plus 7pm Tues and Fri May–Sept), Sat 10.30am only (plus 7pm May–Sept) and last around two hours. For details, tel: 01225 477786.

On Friday evenings you can join a 'ghost walk' around some of the many sites in Bath that are believed to be haunted. Tours (charge made) begin from the Garrick's Head, next to the Theatre Royal (tel: 01225 463618).

Opening times

Though most museums and sights in Bath are open year-round, many attactions in the countryside are open only between March and October or have restricted opening times in winter. Even in summer, some places (such as Dyrham Park and the American Museum) are not open in the morning. Before planning a trip, be sure to check the opening times of the sights you want to see (opening hours are given in the routes section of this guide).

Shops offer late-night shopping on Thursday (normally until 6.30pm, but until 8pm in the run-up to Christmas). Some shops open on Sunday.

Postal services

Main post office

The main post office is in New Bond Street (open Monday to Friday 9am–5.30pm, Saturday 9am–1pm).

Emergencies

Help is at hand

Police, ambulance, fire brigade: 999
Bath Police Station, Manvers Street, tel: 01225 444343
NHS Walk-in Centre, Henry Street (behind Marks and Spencer). Walk-in medical centre open 7am–10pm.
Royal United Hospital, Combe Park, tel: 01225 428331

Disabled access

Though a Georgian city centre doesn't lend itself to access for the disabled, Bath City Council does its best to help. For information on access, contact the Access Officer, tel: 01225 477670.

The Shopmobility Centre, 4 Railway Street (Mon–Fri 9.30am–4.30pm, Saturday 9am–1pm), hires out manual or powered wheelchairs and electric scooters for nominal cost. Book in advance, tel: 01225 481744.

Spectator sports

Rugby

Watch top Rugby Union at the Recreation Ground (near Pulteney Bridge), tel: 01225 460588.

Horse racing

Bath races are held at regular intervals between April and September.

Bath For Children

In spite of its sophisticated image, Bath makes an effort to appeal to children as well as adults. On summer weekends the parks hold regular entertainments, while the river and the Kennet and Avon Canal offer canal and river trips (*see page 71*). The Roman Baths is sufficiently fun to capture the imagination of older children, and the Postal Museum (*see page 28*) appeals to budding philatelists. For children who prefer more active pursuits, Adventure Golf in Royal Victoria Park is the ultimate in crazy golf, while the quasar centre near the bus station can be useful on wet days. Parents with young children should seek out the toyshop Trididas (*see page 69*).

A family day out

The region around Bath offers a wealth of things to do and see. Bristol's hands-on At-Bristol centre (*see page 40*) combines education and fun in its science centre and interactive 'rainforest'. Bristol Zoo (daily 9am–6pm/5pm in winter) and Bristol Ice Rink (tel: 0117 929 2148 for session times) add to the city's attractions. Outdoor tastes are catered for in the Mendip Hills, whose limestone is riddled with caves. The most spectacular of these are Wookey Hole, near Wells (*see page 46*), and Cheddar Showcaves (*see page 45*). At Cheddar children can follow the Crystal Quest or join a caving expedition.

On the Crystal Quest and inside Longleat Safari Park

One of the top regional attractions is Longleat, whose famous safari park is just one of a range of child-oriented attractions (*see page 52*). On the other side of Bath, near Chippenham, is the Castle Combe Skid Pan & Kart Track, where a club for junior drivers is held on the first and third Sunday of every month; tel: 01249 782101. More sedate are the steam railways of the region, including East Somerset Railway at Cranmore (*see page 51*) and the Avon Valley Railway at Bitton (*see page 39*).

All aboard the East Somerset Railway

Accommodation

Booking ahead is essential, especially in summer and on weekends. If you arrive in Bath without accommodation, you can save a lot of legwork by using the Tourist Information Centre's room booking service (charge made: tel: 01225 477101)), though even then you should contact them in advance if you have particular preferences. Failing this, your best bet is to explore Bathwick (over Pulteney Bridge), the Upper Bristol Road or the Wells Road – areas rich in B&Bs. Many of Bath's hotels operate a no-smoking policy and quite a few hotels do not take young children.

Royal Crescent Hotel

The Tourist Information Centre can also supply details of self-catering accommodation. It may also be worth checking out properties of the Landmark Trust (tel: 01628 825925; www.landmarktrust.co.uk), an organisation involved in the restoration and letting of historic buildings. Beckford's Tower *(see page 26)* includes a Landmark Trust flat on its ground floor.

Bath Spa Hotel dining room

City

££££ (over £200 per night double)

Bath Spa Hotel, Sydney Road, tel: 0870 8222; www.bathspahotel.com. Near Sydney Gardens and set in its own extensive grounds. All comforts, including spa..

Priory Hotel, Weston Road, tel: 01225 331922; www.thepriory.co.uk. Gothic-style 18th-century house west of Royal Victoria Park. Comfortable, individual and quiet, with superb restaurant.

The Royal Crescent Hotel, 15–16 The Royal Crescent, tel: 01225 823333; www.royalcrescent.co.uk. The ultimate address in Bath. Antiques, paintings, individually decorated rooms. Secluded garden. Notable restaurant.

£££ (over £120 per night double)

Francis Hotel, Queen Square, tel: 0870 400 8223, tel: 01225 319715; www.macdonaldhotels.co.uk. Occupying another famous address, this time on John Wood the Elder's square, convenient for all the main sights.

The Queensberry Hotel, Russell Street, tel: 01225 447928; www.bathqueensberry.com. Small hotel occupying three Georgian houses knocked together. Comfortable and characterful, though some rooms on the small side. The esteemed Olive Tree restaurant is in the basement.

££ (over £60 double)

Bloomfield House, 146 Bloomfield Road, tel: 01225 420105; www.bloomfield-house.co.uk. B&B in large 19th-century neoclassical house. Some rooms with four-poster or half-tester beds. High up on the south side of Bath, off the Wells Road. Longish walk to the centre. No-smoking.

Dukes Hotel, Great Pulteney Street, tel: 01225 787960, www.dukesbath.co.uk. Comfortable accommodation in Georgian townhouse in one of Bath's finest streets.

Laura Place Hotel, 3 Laura Place, Great Pultney Street, tel: 01225 463815, fax: 01225 310222. Small, characterful hotel in 18th-century building. Good position.

Paradise House Hotel, 86–88 Holloway, tel: 01225-317723; www.paradisehouse.co.uk. Characterful hotel with comfortable rooms, good views and garden. No-smoking.

Sydney Gardens Hotel, Sydney Road, tel: 01225 464818; wwwsydneygardens.co.uk. Comfortable and pretty rooms. No smoking.

Great Pulteney Street

£ (under £60 double)

The Hollies, Hatfield Road, Bath, tel: 01225 313366. Reasonably priced accommodation (all with private bath or shower rooms) in grade II listed Victorian property.

Meadowland, 36 Bloomfield Park, tel: 01225 311079; www.meadowlandbath.co.uk. No Georgian interiors, but very comfortable and well-run. No-smoking.

One of many B&Bs

Outside Bath

££££

Lucknam Park, Colerne (6 miles/10 km from Bath), Wiltshire, tel: 01225 742777; www.lucknampark.co.uk. Luxurious country house/health spa set in 500 acres of parkland. Award-winning restaurant.

£££

Homewood Park Hotel, Hinton, Charterhouse (6 miles/10km from Bath), tel: 01225 723731; www.homewoodpark.com. Country house hotel with good restaurant.

££

Old Manor Hotel, Trowbridge Road, Widbrook, Bradford-on-Avon, tel: 01225 777393; www.oldmanorhotel.com. Sixteenth-century manor farmhouse. Restaurant.

The Old Priory, Church Square, Midsomer Norton, tel: 01761 416784; www.theoldpriory.co.uk. Beautiful medieval priory between Bath and Wells. Michelin-starred restaurant and luxurious accommodation.

Widbrook Grange, Trowbridge Road, Widbrook, Bradford on Avon, tel: 01225 863173; www.widbrookgrange.com. Welcoming small hotel with pleasant rooms, a garden and an indoor pool. No-smoking.

£

The Manor House, Monkton Combe, tel: 01225 723128; www.manorhousebath.co.uk. 16th-century manor offering reasonably priced accommodation (private facilities). Breakfast served until noon.

Index